11/04

Genius Denied

How to Stop Wasting Our
Brightest Young Minds

Jan and Bob Davidson
with Laura Vanderkam

SIMON & SCHUSTER

New York   London   Toronto   Sydney

SIMON & SCHUSTER
Rockefeller Center
1230 Avenue of the Americas
New York, NY 10020

For information about special discounts for bulk purchases,
please contact Simon & Schuster Special Sales:
1-800-456-6798 or business@simonandschuster.com

Manufactured in the United States of America

10   9   8   7   6   5   4   3   2   1

Library of Congress Cataloging-in-Publication Data

Davidson, Jan.
    Genius Denied / Jan and Bob Davidson with Laura Vanderkam.
        p. cm.
    Includes bibliographical references and index.
        1. Gifted children—Education—United States. I. Davidson, Bob, date.–.
    II. Vanderkam, Laura. III. Title.

    LC3993.9.D37 2004
    371.95—dc22
                                                              2003065905

ISBN 0-7432-5460-0

FIRST, WE WISH TO THANK the students, parents, and educators affiliated with the Davidson Institute for Talent Development for sharing their stories with us. They told us this book needed to be written, and their generous contribution of anecdotes, research, and time made this book possible. To protect their privacy, we have changed many of the children's names, but not the details of their lives. These families and educators inspire us in our mission to develop the talent of America's brightest students.

This book also was supported and influenced by every member of our Davidson Institute team. These talented professionals helped us find the research we needed, helped us clarify our communications, and encouraged us at every point along the way. In particular we wish to acknowledge Marie Capurro, Julie Dudley, Katie Graham, Colleen Harsin, Crissa Haynes, Brennan Johnson, Abby Jones, Travis Rabe, Amy Williams, and Jonathan Wilson.

We received feedback and guidance from several experts in the field of gifted education as this book evolved. In particular, we would like to thank Susan Assouline, Nicholas Colangelo, Tracy Cross, Jim Delisle, Miraca Gross, Sidney Moon, Paula Olszewski-Kubilius, Nancy Robinson, and Joyce VanTassel-Baska. We are grateful for the contributions of Jane Clarenbach at the National Association for Gifted Children, Sandra Berger at the Council for Exceptional Children, Rena Subotnik at the American Psychological Association, and Linda Brody at the Johns Hopkins Center for Talented Youth. This book relied heavily on the work of numerous researchers in the fields of psychology and education. Whenever we needed additional details, they were graciously provided. We are especially indebted to our friend Dr. Julian Stanley, founder of the Johns Hopkins Center for Talented Youth. His work in identifying and nurturing intellectual talent has shaped our mission and our lives.

When we first decided to write a book on gifted education, we approached our good friends Dick Snyder and Laura Yorke to ask for their opinions. Dick and Laura's wise advice gleaned from years in the publishing industry, their enthusiasm for the book, and their feedback on structure and content helped us move from idea to manuscript. Many thanks to our agent, Carol Mann of the Carol Mann Agency, for her guidance in the development of this book and for securing its placement with Simon & Schuster. Bob Bender, senior editor at Simon & Schuster, is a superb editor and advocate. We are grateful for his guidance and advice, and for the help of his assistant, Johanna Li. We worked with Simon & Schuster over a decade ago to copublish several Davidson & Associates educational software titles, so we value the opportunity once again to be associated with the company's talented team of professionals.

We wish to thank Laura Vanderkam for her contribution as the writer of this book. Laura is not only a talented young writer, but as a gifted young person herself, she brought to the book her own unique perspective and understanding of the obstacles our society sometimes places upon its brightest young citizens. Our relationship with Laura in the creation of this book made the process particularly satisfying. We greatly value her contribution and the friendship that has evolved from our working together. She wishes to thank *USA Today* Forum page editors Chris Collins and Glen Nishimura for publishing her column on radical acceleration, "Some Can Sail Over High School," in

August 2002. That column caught our attention and led to this writing partnership.

Many thanks to our family and friends for taking an interest in our work and politely listening as we have talked about *Genius Denied* for the past two years. In particular we thank our children, Liz, Emilie, and John, who continually help us grow as people and as parents.

Jan and Bob Davidson

This book is dedicated to the
Davidson Fellows,
Davidson Young Scholars,
and their parents, teachers, and mentors.
You inspire us and enrich our lives.

Contents

Genius Denied

At the Davidson Institute for Talent Development, a nonprofit organization we founded in 1999 to help our nation's brightest children get the education they need, we're always amazed by the stories families share with us. We receive an e-mail from a mother who describes how her son, at age two, learned all the state capitals as an afternoon diversion and later solved three-digit arithmetic problems when he was bored in his stroller. We smile at the story of another toddler who tried to weasel out of trouble for throwing a toy back at his sibling by claiming he was just following "Newton's Third Law." A ten-year-old composes a set of complex piano pieces. A teenager pursues a patent on an antibody he developed to slow the growth of tumors.

Sadly, not all the stories we hear make us smile. Most tell how schools and communities neglect these highly intelligent children. They are kept with children their own age, rarely given work that challenges them, and told they will just have to learn to work at the same pace as everyone else. We hear of children who read and comprehend their math books in the first two weeks of school and spend the rest of the year gazing out the window. Teenagers who read Dostoyevsky for pleasure suffer the tedium of classes that devote weeks to books written for young adult audiences.

This book is about their stories. We have changed these children's names, but not the details of the difficulties they have encountered trying to eke out an appropriate education. This book is about whether schools and communities choose to squelch or nurture the flame of intelligence in their young people, and what happens when they choose to deny or embrace this national resource. Learning becomes a joy when children have what we call "aha!" moments. An equation works, a story makes sense, and a little connection forges in a child's brain. The harder a child has to work to make that connection, the brighter the lightbulb burns.

People always ask us why, when we sold Davidson & Associates, our educational software company, and entered the world of philanthropy, we chose to work with gifted children. Our reply is that we have always wanted to help children become successful learners. Even before founding Davidson & Associates, Jan taught English at the college level and tutored children of all ages. Bob's ideas for our math and reading software helped thousands of students discover that learning can be as much fun as playing video games. We want all children to have these "aha!" moments. So we searched for the population that traditional schools serve least, the population that is least likely to learn and achieve to its potential. We believe that highly gifted students are that population.

Over the years, we have discovered that when it comes to leaving no child behind, highly gifted students are the most likely to fall through the cracks in American classrooms. They are the most likely to underachieve, to suffer the greatest gap between their potential and what is asked of them. This is what we mean by "genius denied."

"Genius" means extraordinary intellectual ability, and people use the word in two different but related ways. In one sense, genius means high intellectual potential; in the other sense, genius means "creative ability of exceptionally high order as demonstrated by total achievement." This book uses both meanings. Works of eminence require years of preparation and require minds working to the best of their abilities. If we fail to recognize and nurture extraordinary intellectual ability in our children, we will deny them the opportunity to develop their talents to their full extent and deny them, and the nation, the satisfaction and benefits of what these children may someday do.

At the Davidson Institute we try to help highly gifted young people find ways to keep learning to the extent of their abilities. Our Davidson Young Scholars program provides guidance, resources, and educational advocacy assistance to hundreds of families of talented young people ages four to eighteen. Our Davidson Fellows award program provides scholarships to students who already have completed works of great importance. Our Educators Guild provides teachers with resources and training to identify and nurture gifted students in their classrooms. And we grant awards to schools with an exemplary record for nurturing intellectual talent.

We are writing this book to share the stories of the children, families, and teachers we have met through these programs, and to help readers understand how schools deny these "aha!" moments to bright students by failing to challenge them. We do not believe that most educators or schools or communities are hostile to the needs of gifted learners. Rather, most people are simply indifferent. With all the other educational crises plaguing American schools these days, why, people ask, should we focus on children who seem better able than other students to fend for themselves? People believe these children have it easy. They ace tests without trying. They race through their homework.

We first answer these questions by saying that schools should not discriminate against gifted kids. All kids—low-achievers, high-achievers, and those in the middle—deserve to have their educational needs met. But we also have another reason for wanting schools and society to nurture gifted children. Through our work we have met young people who have composed symphonies, written novels, made advancements in the treatment of cancer, and found new ways of compressing data for faster and cheaper storage and retrieval, all before they were old enough to vote. These young people benefited from parents, teachers, mentors, and communities that supported and encouraged them. Unlike so many of their talented peers, their genius was nurtured, not denied. We want to live in a world where such talent is harnessed and put to use. We can't expect to benefit from gifted children's creativity later if we let schools dull their minds into indifference now.

The simple solution, it seems to us, is to make sure that gifted children, like all other children, are given material that is challenging enough to allow them to learn. We also know that children learn best when surrounded by their intellectual peers. Yet in a country with one hundred types of toothpaste on supermarket shelves, schools still follow a one-size-fits-all educational model. Children march in lockstep through grades with their age peers, regardless of their capabilities. Changing schools so they focus on whether a child reaches her potential—instead of focusing on whether she passes the standardized test and spends 180 days in a seat—will require a major shift in thinking for parents, teachers, administrators, and policy makers.

It won't be easy, but it is a cause worth fighting for. Such individualized education will make school more humane for all students and, particularly in the case of gifted students, will reap rewards for society for years to come.

The first three chapters of *Genius Denied* discuss the problem—how schools shortchange their brightest students, even in gifted programs, and how America's lowest-common-denominator culture has created this educational neglect. The next four chapters show how parents, teachers, mentors, patrons, schools, and society can help gifted students achieve their potential. A *What You Can Do* section at the back of the book provides practical suggestions for nurturing your own gifted child or other gifted children in your community.

In five years at the Davidson Institute we have met hundreds of highly gifted students through our programs. We know these students can do anything if given the chance. In America today, however, too few schools take that chance. They prefer instead to live with the consequences of genius denied.

Chapter 1

Genius Denied

WHEN RACHEL was four years old, she told her mother she wanted to write a story. The little girl couldn't physically write the words yet, so she asked her mother to write them down for her. Her mother agreed to do so and then marveled as Rachel dictated an elaborate ten-page tale called "The Time of Great Recise" about a recently orphaned heroine struggling with her grief. Rachel knew no word that meant "strife," but also the process of overcoming it, so she coined "recise" to mean just that. She was too young and her ideas too big to be limited by the English language.

For Rachel, growing up in a small town in Pennsylvania, writing proved to be her own means of "great recise." She was always different. When she played with other children her age, she wanted to talk about her Chronicles of Narnia books and the science fiction fantasy worlds she dreamed up, while they wanted to talk about toys. Troubled by this, she looked forward to school. She imagined there would be other children like her there—children who vacuumed up information, children who had hundreds of questions, children who loved to solve fascinating problems. So she watched the school bus from the window and looked forward to all she would learn.

But school, too, lagged behind her mind. Rachel knew how to read already and read voraciously. By second grade the rest of her class was reading two-paragraph selections from a reader while she raced through the comprehension questions to devour a few more pages in her Madeleine L'Engle books. She used words her classmates didn't understand, so she was the quirky child. In elementary school that was mostly okay. She came to class dressed as Jo March to tell the other eight-year-olds the plot of *Little Women,* and she soaked up their rapt attention. She produced a science fiction trilogy of short stories that earned her a place in her school's gifted program, although all that meant was a few extra hours a week of word puzzles and the like. She read books on everything from politics to physics and formed opinions on world affairs that seemed strange coming from a curly-haired child. And some force kept compelling her to write. She would skip anything else to make the words that jumbled in her head appear on the page.

Rachel's parents knew she was a high-maintenance child— energetic, emotional, and very, very bright. Then they had her tested and discovered that her IQ (intelligence quotient) was so high, a score like hers occurred less than once in a thousand people. A small town like hers might encounter such a child in its elementary school every few years at most. Rachel's frenetic mind was years older than her body.

While it was a comfort to have their suspicions confirmed, Rachel's parents worried about the rest of her schooling. Would officials, administrators, and teachers work with them to meet her needs? They soon learned how difficult and hostile school can be for a child who is different.

The trouble began when Rachel started middle school. Every

night she scribbled and typed a bit more for a novel, an arching saga that swelled to four hundred pages. Meanwhile, at school, her English teacher insisted that the class circle nouns in sentences, and then she sent everyone home with more worksheets of the same. The pointlessness of it stunned Rachel. She had to take time from writing about other galaxies to underscore verbs. She began to dread the wasted hours.

Then there was the matter of social hierarchy, which grew more important with every passing year. Rachel talked too much in class. She wanted to argue points with the teachers and other children. She couldn't cope with lunchroom conversations about clothes and boys and the tedious matter of who sat next to whom. She was always on the outside. Middle school dances and parties—she'd rather be writing. When sentences stirred in her brain, her thoughts dashed inward, away from everything else.

She mourned having no one to share her love of words with, but so it went. While her teacher assigned a list of spelling words for students to study, she wrote her own stories under the desk. She read everything she could on science and threw herself into a distance-learning writing course from Johns Hopkins University. And every year she looked forward to a monthlong summer canoeing trip as part of a wilderness program in Canada. There, in groups of eight girls, she eased the pressure on her mind by pushing her body to its limits. The outdoors didn't stifle her like a classroom. She slowly grew in confidence with the help of fellow wayfarers who accepted her as she was.

That was four weeks a year, however. The rest of the time grew worse and worse. By tenth grade the meaningless work assigned simply to keep everyone busy made her despair. It became a routine, like an assembly line: Read the stilted prose of a biology book and answer the end-of-chapter questions. Spend weeks wading through what happens in an assigned novel instead of discussing what it means. Memorize the names of medieval kings. Cough them up on a quiz and forget them. Rachel could see no end to it. Her parents asked for special courses or distance-learning opportunities, but the school refused. It had never been done before, administrators said. The school wouldn't count her Johns Hopkins writing courses toward her diploma, so she kept taking English classes that dwelt on sentence structure as she wrote long stories every ten days at home. She raced through school books, then read *The Brothers Karamazov* and *Anna Karenina* under her desk.

The school did promise that she could take college courses in her junior year, but not a moment sooner and only if she took certain prerequisites. Simply testing out of these prerequisites would not be allowed. So she waded through "technical education" and took so many classes that one term she didn't have a lunch break. She packaged lunches in bits that she could eat in the halls. Students weren't allowed to eat in the halls, and she often got in trouble for that.

Being exiled from the cafeteria only increased her social isolation. She couldn't fit into her small-town high school's world of homecoming queens, high school fashions, and locker gossip. To fill lonely hours on nights and weekends, she worked more than she needed to. A teacher assigned a ten-page story in English, and she wrote a twenty-eight-page novella called *I-Ana* on string theory and canoeing. She hoped the college classes to come would tap that jumble of ideas inside her head, a jumble that had nowhere to go and was slowly driving her crazy.

But then she saw the list of college courses offered. All introductory classes. Sciences that were offered at the high school were not allowed. No physics, no psychology. Mostly things she knew. She asked for an exception to choose from the course catalogue. The school refused to grant it. It had never been done before, they said. The local college refused to help without her high school's permission. Those were the rules, they said, and there was nothing anyone could do.

After that, Rachel started falling apart. She was tired of jumping through hoops. She felt herself shrinking, she said, as the world of her high school pressed in on her. What did classes matter when she knew everything taught in them? Not learning made her miserable. She decided that she was the crazy one, that she was too different. It was better to stop trying. She started getting C's on her report cards. She became even more withdrawn, writing about her demons and the futility of life. Her listlessness terrified her parents. They took her to a psychologist. Severe depression was the diagnosis—the depression of an ambitious child who flies straight into a brick wall.

Children with learning disabilities are by law given "individual education plans" to address their specific learning needs; some districts do the same for gifted children. Acknowledging Rachel's exceptional intelligence, the school drew up an individual education plan for her. As part of it, some teachers created a behavioral checklist for her in tenth grade. It was a prescription for how to fit in: Don't talk so much in class; keep it to a sound bite. Don't be so aggressive. Don't answer all the questions. Don't discuss things so much. Tone it down. Don't challenge the classroom status quo.

There it was, written down for her to follow: how to take that precocious mind and learn to be like everyone else.

* * *

Joshua played the piano with a brilliance that defied his tiny body. At age two he saw his uncle perform and told his mother he wanted to try. Even as a toddler he never banged his hands against the keyboard. He played notes on their own, concentrating on the sounds. Though normally an active little boy, he could sit patiently on the piano bench for half an hour or more, mesmerized by the shiny black and white keys. He played and played, and he got better, jumping from "Mary Had a Little Lamb" to Mozart like leaping from puddle to puddle. His feet couldn't reach the pedals. Yet when Joshua was five, his teacher convinced his parents, Margaret and Vladislav, that their son might qualify for admission to the Juilliard School's pre-college program. They brought him to the grand building behind the Lincoln Center in New York City and let him play for the judges. Joshua and his teacher had to choose music that wouldn't suffer because his fingers couldn't yet reach an octave, but he passed the audition anyway. He became the youngest child ever admitted. He and his mother began making the pilgrimage to Manhattan every Saturday, following the other little prodigies into Juilliard's halls.

Meanwhile, during the week Joshua attended a normal public elementary school in suburban New York. His precocity extended beyond the piano. He learned to read before starting school. His immigrant parents assumed school would be like playing the piano—you moved ahead as quickly as you learned. It wasn't. When Joshua finished assignments long before the rest of the class, his first grade teacher told him to keep quiet at his desk. The little boy had a hard time sitting still without a piano in front of him. He talked to the other children and tried to make them laugh, and he wound up in the principal's office at least once a week for causing trouble. Margaret met with Joshua's teacher and asked her to give him more work—something to read, something to do. The teacher instead turned these meetings into a litany of Joshua's behavioral faults. He had to learn to behave and cope with boredom. Nobody got anything special. Everyone had to do the same thing. So Joshua kept going to the principal's office, learning early on that being different made him bad.

Joshua's family lived in a good school district. People bought houses there because the schools promised to expose children to a wide variety of opportunities. One of those opportunities was music class, which was required every year. It wasn't quite Juilliard. Margaret later learned that the elementary school music teacher once ran to another teacher in tears after class because, as she said, "I don't know what to do. Joshua can teach me." At this time Joshua was making his concerto debut, playing Haydn's D-Major Piano Concerto with the New York String Society. But this didn't matter. Joshua couldn't go to another room to play the piano during music class or even sit in the corner and read. He had to spend hours clapping the rhythm for quarter notes and other things he had learned long ago.

Joshua's school, like Rachel's, had a gifted program, of sorts. It was open to any reasonably bright child who showed an interest, and it consisted of little more than puzzles and extra work in addition to the worksheets and end-of-chapter comprehension questions. Joshua barely had time for that because of his hours of daily piano practice and his weekends filled with lessons. He loved piano; his face would light up as he talked of his favorite piece, a concerto by Shostakovich. It had a simple structure, he said, a little of everything, and it was a bit out there, though not so out there as something by John Cage, though of course Beethoven was considered out there for his time. Perhaps classical in the sense of Rachmaninoff, whose showiness hid a classical construction. Composers' names and styles flowed off the boy's tongue.

The children at Juilliard he saw once a week shared this fascination, but not the children at his middle school. There, people didn't understand his lack of interest in sports and his frustration with the school's militant devotion to grade-level and only grade-level work. Over the years his friends dwindled in number as they had less and less to talk about. He went through the same awkwardness as other thirteen-year-olds, made worse by the precocity that already made him different. The three to four hours of daily practice wore him down, too. With long, boring school days already filled with mindless distractions, he had little time for anything else. He grew tired of being different, tired of not fitting in. And, increasingly, he began to suffer from stage fright. In the past, Joshua had played at benefit concerts in full halls. He even played the role of a young Beethoven in an *A&E Biography* series, performing music by Mozart and Haydn. Now he became petrified of failing before thousands of people. He had seldom been truly challenged, and so he had never failed at anything. The possibility made his knees go weak.

He considered quitting the piano. His mother said he could if he wanted to. She just wanted him to feel normal, she said. Joshua didn't like being so different, either. So one of the world's most promising young musicians considered leaving his first love.

■ Squandered Talent, Wasted Time

Rachel and Joshua are real children. In small-town Pennsylvania and suburban New York they discovered that for gifted students like themselves, school can be an act of mental cruelty—or at best a waste of time. They are just two of thousands of such precocious, frustrated children nationwide who have watched the educational establishment shrug at their special gifts. They have seen their zeal for discovery buried in inertia. They wonder why school has to be so boring and why learning can't be more of a joy.

Every day we hear tales of their troubles. One teenage girl tells of being mocked as a "rocket scientist" by a teacher trying to gain rapport with a class. A mother is told to put her child on Ritalin to drug the boredom away. An eager, extroverted six-year-old girl has to be dragged to school because she dreads the dull hours so much. A seventh grade boy learns algebra over the summer, but has to repeat the class in eighth grade because his school can't be bothered with accommodating his new knowledge. Schools label some gifted children as dull troublemakers because they refuse to do meaningless work. Others simply endure social isolation for speaking differently and caring about things different from other children their age.

While many gifted children eventually triumph in their quest to learn, few have an easy time of it. Indeed, we know that most highly gifted children are chronic underachievers—doing enough to get straight A's, but hardly enough to stretch and grow their minds. Gifted education pioneer Leta Hollingworth once wrote that "in the ordinary elementary school situation, children of 140 IQ waste half their time. Those of 170 IQ waste practically all their time." Except for a few bright spots, the situation has only worsened since Hollingworth conducted her research in the 1920s and 1930s. In America today the educational system—which is focused on the lowest common denominator—is more likely to crush a bright child's spirit than nurture her intellect.

Two realities drive these children's torments. First, America prides itself on being an egalitarian nation. The highly gifted seem privileged and thus undeserving of help. In tight times, funding for gifted education becomes a luxury. Massachusetts, for example, recently slashed an already meager gifted education budget from roughly $400,000 a year to zero. California's then-Governor Gray Davis vetoed a 2002 bill that would have helped gifted students attend college early, because the state is required to provide a free education for all children through age eighteen: He claimed it was too expensive. The 2002 federal education budget allotted only $11 million for gifted programs, and this was mostly for research projects, not classroom instruction. President Bush's No Child Left Behind Act of 2001 increased educational spending—but almost entirely for those on the lower end of the achievement ladder. Overall, researcher Joyce Van Tassel-Baska estimates, America spends 143 times more on special education than gifted education.

Money alone won't make children learn, although it helps. But even well-funded schools suffer from the second problem: America has also become an anti-intellectual nation. When Harvard University lowers its standards to recruit students who can win football games or capture championships in women's squash, it's no surprise that the rest of the country is prepared to compromise on academic achievement. If you walk into any American high school, the trophies you see displayed in the hall case are unlikely to be those of the student who won the state math contest. USA Today's annual All-USA Academic lists showcase students with significant community service achievements more than those whose contributions have advanced human knowledge.

Evidence of this neglect rolls in. American businesses lament the shortage of highly skilled workers, and universities import many scientists and engineers from abroad. The number of American students scoring above 1000 on the SAT declined so much over the past few decades that the test had to be adjusted to "recenter"—and thus raise—the scores. Observers note that standard textbooks have declined as much as two grade levels in complexity since early in the twentieth century. Princeton University recently instituted basic writing classes to assist some of the highest-achieving kids in America who show up at college unable to write essays.

Quite simply, schools do not challenge their most intelligent students. And not only do they not challenge their gifted students, they push them back toward the middle, lauding doctrines of "socialization" and radical egalitarianism, which deny that some children learn faster than others. As we hear again and again from gifted kids who are forced to stare at the clock as they wait for their classmates to catch up, schools teach bright students that curiosity only makes you miserable. The Higher Education Research Institute's 2001 survey of college freshmen found that an all-time high of 41 percent reported being frequently bored in high school. And HERI's 2002 survey found that while nearly 46 percent received A averages, fewer students than ever did even an hour's worth of homework each night.

■ Defining the Gifted

Even some advocates for highly intelligent students have let problems of defining "giftedness" stand in the way of meeting these children's needs.

Most gifted programs in America concern themselves less with matching an appropriate curriculum to the child than with identifying a few students, either by IQ or achievement test scores or teacher recommendations, and giving them a few hours a week of enrichment activities. Because these programs need a cutoff point, schools or districts create one. Many use IQ scores, since IQ tests do offer a good, albeit not perfect, view of a person's capacity to learn and his or her problem-solving ability. But because a child with an IQ of 121 is not appreciably brighter than one with an IQ of 119, critics of gifted education can easily point out the absurdity. And advocates have accepted these limited programs in order to ease the highly gifted student's boredom for a few hours, rather than demand that education be reformed to challenge all students, particularly the brightest, to the extent of their abilities.

Few schools understand differences in precocity among gifted children. As many as one in six American students between the ages of four and eighteen—some 10 million young people—receive this label for scoring one standard deviation or more above the norm on intelligence tests. These tests, such as the Wechsler Intelligence Scale for Children, assign scores based on how thousands of people answer various questions. The average IQ score is 100 with a standard deviation of 15 points. Sixty percent of the population falls within one standard deviation either way (85–115); 95 percent fall within the 70–130 range. A score of seventy indicates borderline retardation. The qualification for school gifted programs ranges from 115 to 130, depending on the state. A score of 145 occurs in the population roughly once in one thousand, while a score of 160 occurs in the population once in ten thousand.

While children with IQs of 120 or 160 may both be called "gifted," they learn at different rates and think at very different levels. This wide range of intellectual abilities includes students who may be satisfied with moderate academic advancement, such as taking algebra in eighth grade, and more intellectually advanced students who may be ready for calculus in elementary school. It covers students who read just a bit above grade level and twelve-year-olds who devour Tolstoy by flashlight under the covers at night. Yet educational policies tend to view the gifted as a homogeneous group and assume that any gifted program put in place will satisfy all these children's needs.

It won't. Few schools, even well-funded suburban ones, offer highly gifted children an appropriate education, even within their gifted programs. In Joshua's and Rachel's schools the gifted programs offered puzzles or games or just additional, inappropriate work. Honors classes meant moving ahead a bit, but not enough to challenge children capable of thinking years beyond their age. Even moderately gifted children are shortchanged by schools that care only about the percentages of students who pass the state's assessment tests.

We recognize the special needs of all these students. However, as we see daily, the brighter the child, the more likely he or she will suffer in a school that teaches to the middle. The problem becomes most acute in what we call "highly gifted" students, which in educational parlance means IQs of at least 145 or roughly three standard deviations above the norm. These are the students who score above average for high school seniors when they take the SAT through talent searches as middle schoolers. They score at the 99th percentile on grade-level standardized tests whether they've paid attention in class or not. They learn to read early and can comprehend chapter books intended for older children within a few months of learning their letters. Most are fascinated by numbers and will flip ahead in their math books or borrow an older sibling's textbooks to figure out what wonderful things they can do to solve these problems.

The U.S. Department of Education defines giftedness by saying: "Children and youth with outstanding talent perform or show the potential for performing at remarkably high levels of accomplishment when compared with others of their age, experience, and environment."

Highly gifted students show potential for performing at re-markably high levels compared with other *good* students of the same age, experience, and environment. In good schools mildly gifted students tend to do well and work a bit for their grades. But even in good schools, most highly gifted children do not re-ceive work challenging enough to stretch their minds. Failing to meet these students needs because of the hazards of defining giftedness is like failing to feed the hungry because people quib-ble over how many calories the body requires.

Students with the most potential are at the greatest risk of underachievement in an educational system that still believes in grouping children by age, not ability. During our years of work-ing with highly intelligent students, we have seen that they need constant mental stimulation due to the rapid rate at which they learn. They need to explore a subject in depth in order to under-stand the "why" and the "how" as well as the "what." They learn little or nothing from regurgitating information on worksheets or providing answers to end-of-chapter questions, even if they copy the questions themselves, as many teachers stalling for time insist they do. When kept with children their own age and told to wait for everyone else to catch up, the brightest students strain at their constraints the way most adults would if told they had to return to the sixth grade. To keep from going crazy, highly gifted students learn to stunt their own growth in order not to appear different. They miss out on those "aha!" moments of discovery that make learning such a joy. They fail to develop the discipline and confidence that comes from being challenged to the extent of their abilities.

But these missed opportunities aren't just a tragedy for gifted kids and their families. Stunting the growth of gifted children means quietly limiting the ability of society to make the great leaps in art and science that will benefit us all. "What is honored in a country will be cultivated there," Plato wrote, and the societies we remember in history tend to be the ones that nurtured genius from their ranks. Plato's own classical Athens, Renaissance Florence, and Elizabethan England sparkle in history because works by such masters as Euripedes, Aristotle, Michelangelo, da Vinci, Shakespeare, Marlowe, and others have influenced and lasted far beyond their creators' lives. These societies nurtured genius through master teachers, patrons, and artistic freedom. In return, these creative masters assured their societies' contributions to the pursuit of truth.

Conditions were not perfect. Reactionaries shuddered at new ideas; officials forced Socrates to drink hemlock after convicting him of corrupting youth. Shortsighted leaders ignored minorities and the underclass and dismissed women's talents and minds. These societies focused almost all their resources on educating a few well-to-do men. America, on the other hand, is committed to educating everyone. In this our schools have been somewhat successful. Most Americans can read, write, and perform enough arithmetic functions to hold a wide variety of jobs and participate in society.

But commitment to that goal doesn't mean basic education is a ceiling. It is a floor from which children should leap as high as they can. Shakespeare didn't spend his youth writing five-paragraph essays, and it would have been ridiculous to expect him to do so.

We can combine the best of our system with the intellectual cultures of these societies that nurtured genius. America has the potential to stand out from history even more than Athens, Florence, and Elizabethan England because we don't acknowledge the talents of only a narrow segment of society—white and male. We have an even bigger pool of talent, and our capabilities are greater because of that.

It is the gifted children of today who will make the future scientific and medical contributions that will someday improve lives. It is these children who will write novels and compose symphonies that will someday move souls. As Dr. Julian Stanley, founder of the Center for Talented Youth at Johns Hopkins, says, "If we want these young people to be prepared when society needs them, we need to be there for them when they need us." If we can nurture the talent of the brilliant children we've met in all walks of life—such as a little girl on a North Dakota air force base, a boy in an isolated Alaska town, and immigrant children newly arrived in this country—we are better off than if we trust that a few good prep schools in New England will do the job with the children of America's wealthiest citizens.

But instead we squander our own deep vein of talent by failing to nurture talented students such as Joshua and Rachel. Because of our culture's obsession with all children doing the same thing at the same time, Joshua's all-American school required the youngest child ever admitted to Juilliard to clap out quarter notes in music class. Rachel's school preferred finding fault with her behavior to thinking that maybe circling nouns didn't capture a budding novelist's imagination.

That leveling impulse also led educators years ago to make public schools imitate factories where everyone comes out the same. Even in the information age, old habits die hard. In many districts, school means sticking a child on the assembly line at age five and shuffling him through 180-day years of hourly bells, lockers, and repetition until he emerges at age eighteen "educated." By design and often by ideology, such schools are unable to nurture children who cannot think inside the box.

Some people find this a fair deal. Education is "the great equalizer," Horace Mann said, and many people believe that social justice means keeping all children of the same age together, teaching them the same things, concentrating all special attention and extra resources on those who need help to catch up, and trusting that gifted children will fend for themselves.

We disagree. True social justice means providing an education that challenges all students to the extent of their abilities—gifted children included. Blessed with brilliant minds and enormous skill, these highly intelligent students may not seem to warrant much help, but they have special needs, too. They deserve far more attention than America's education system currently offers them. The nation's future depends on their energies and talents, and wasting their childhoods because of inertia, ignorance, or ideology is as shortsighted as writing off children because of religion or race.

*   *   *

We want to call attention to the quiet crisis that comes from dulling the minds of children such as Rachel and Joshua. Through the children we meet, we learn daily how schools shortchange America's brightest youth and how much these children can do when given the chance. Imagine a seven-year-old boy who redesigns the carbon dioxide recovery system of the Apollo spacecraft. Imagine a ten-year-old girl who writes science fiction novels. Imagine a teenager whose mathematical modeling of gasoline sprays and direct-injection technology influences the automobile industry. Then imagine these children stuck in classrooms where they're forced to color worksheets to pass the hours and told to stop complaining if they're bored.

It doesn't have to be this way. We think of the story of a young woman we know named Brennan who grew up on a hog farm in Delhi, Iowa. Slopping pigs and chasing after piglets, she learned early how to work hard with her brothers and parents to keep the farm running. Brennan always asked questions. She loved learning about the world by playing in a cabin she and her brothers built in the woods, acting out adventure stories, and pretending she was an explorer.

Then she started elementary school, and soon realized how different she was. First, as a biracial child, hers was the only dark face in an all-white class. Then she discovered that the other children didn't learn to read so fast and didn't find their curiosity pricked the way she did by everything she read. Brennan's parents had her tested. Her scores showed she had mastered material several grade levels above her age. The school wasn't sure what to do. All the lower elementary school children worked from reading kits coded by different colors for different levels. So Brennan received a reading kit that was a different color from all the other children and was told to work through it by herself. For two years she did this, teaching herself what she could. No one checked up on her. After two years the school tested her again. She didn't do as well as she thought she would, but that result made her happy. Now she was no longer different, she thought. Now she no longer had to be the strange child working alone.

Then when she was eight, her parents divorced. Her mom found a job in a truck-parts factory, so Brennan and two of her brothers moved with her. They struggled financially on her mother's wages. When her mother quit her job to return to school, the family went on welfare. Brennan's mother would rise at 6 A.M. on Sundays to redeem her food stamps at the local supermarket—so no one she knew would see her. The family lived in a housing complex where drunks regularly caused commotions, children were often neglected, and a neighbor was arrested for molesting his daughter.

Brennan's father didn't fare much better. He worked a third shift at a plastics factory. His house had little heat. When Brennan spent the night, she had to sleep under piles of blankets to stay warm.

Brennan soon learned that everyone in the small town where she lived knew the low-rent district she lived in and knew how her family got by. When her mom sent her to buy small necessities with food stamps, her best friend refused to go anywhere near her.

Poverty didn't stunt Brennan's intellect, though. As it is for many gifted children, seventh grade was the turning point. She played clarinet in the school band and, with little practice, won first chair. She earned straight A's with little effort. But Brennan grew frustrated with the lack of challenge. Although she loved hands-on work, she endured science classes without labs. Her literature classes spent weeks reading books aloud, every student reading a paragraph by turn. She could finish and comprehend these books in a night. Even though she excelled in athletics, generally a ticket to popularity, she felt perpetually on the outside, not sure whether her outsider status was the result of her skin color, poverty, intelligence, or all three. "I had one seventh grade teacher who told me that I was going to be a real success, but no one else had too much faith in me," Brennan says.

She tried to challenge herself as best she could. Seeking a new sport, she went out for the football team, which scandalized some school traditionalists. She battled for admission to a University of Iowa summer program for gifted students. Around the time she won her school's one slot, someone wrote a note about her, using the "n-word" and saying she did not know her place. She discovered that she no longer knew whom she could sit with at lunch. People whispered about her in the halls, and she realized that she was too different for some people to tolerate.

Fortunately, she moved again the next year when her mom

found a job in Des Moines. Des Moines had a gifted program that actually provided students with fully challenging classes from middle school on, at a place called the Central Academy at Central Campus. Central "celebrated learning," Brennan says. Her test scores gained her admission to the half-day program, and for five years she went to Central and her regular school every day. She reveled in Advanced Placement chemistry, biology, and physics classes, and worked through the advanced math and humanities courses, earning so many credits that she became an AP Scholar with Distinction. Still she struggled with feeling different as she boarded the bus at lunchtime. At her first middle school, she dealt with an urban culture of drugs and teen pregnancy that was new to her. Then at her high school the discipline improved, but she discovered that the racial issue never went away. There, some black students accused her of "acting white" for going to a supposedly elitist school.

But Brennan wanted to go to college, a good college somewhere far from Iowa, so she stayed with it. She discovered she had a knack for science. When a teacher at Central announced a research internship at Iowa State University, Brennan seized the opportunity. She applied and was accepted. The summer before her senior year she spent two weeks with a professor on an island in the middle of the Mississippi studying the effect of temperature on sex determination in turtles. They tagged eggs, watched the females, and collected data, bringing Brennan partly back to life on the farm. The fun and challenge whetted her appetite for more.

Back at the university, the internship required an independent research project. Brennan decided to document the evolutionary history of the hognose snake by studying scale samples. She threw herself into learning the lab techniques to do so.

In the course of her research she found a sample that could

not be explained with the others. She tried different hypotheses. Once the internship ended, she continued her research. She hunted down environmental reasons for the different DNA. She pored over books on taxonomy and mitochondrial DNA sequencing. She studied the snake's habitat to determine whether ice-age barriers had separated family lines of the snake. By January she had worked out her theory: It turned out that she had discovered a new subspecies. Her research results won her widespread attention and helped her gain admission to Columbia University in New York City, a universe away from the isolated hog farm in Delhi and her small-town educational frustrations.

Brennan was smart enough to accomplish anything, but she needed people to recognize that potential, and a school system and community that was wise enough to value bright young people and challenge them to use their gifts. All highly gifted young people need this support.

Brennan was lucky. Without her mother's new job, she might have stayed in a school district that couldn't or wouldn't help her. In some ways Joshua and Rachel were lucky, too. Rachel had teachers who gave her books from the school storeroom and winked as she devised guerrilla assignments, such as translating sonnets, in place of homework that didn't interest her. Rachel's parents cared enough to seek opportunities even if her school wouldn't, and they were vigilant enough to make sure she got help when school started to drive her mad. They also recognized the true nature of the problem. With their encouragement, Rachel submitted her *I-Ana* manuscript to the American Psychological Association's Pinnacle program and landed a mentorship with novelists Jonathan and Faye Kellerman. She applied for and won a full scholarship to Simon's Rock College of Bard in tenth grade and so escaped the confines of her high school two years early. Simon's Rock helped disperse her depression like clouds.

As for Joshua, he lives in suburban New York, and his musical gifts can be nurtured at Juilliard even if only for one day a week. He can play a concerto with the Metropolitan Youth Orchestra before a rapt audience, and he can go to Juilliard master classes, practice a few minutes beforehand, and then sit down and play Chopin's Revolutionary Etude so perfectly that it leaves even him shaking and smiling. These things make the long weeks more tolerable and remind him that his gift is worth more than the trials of being different.

But imagine if Joshua had lived elsewhere. Imagine if Rachel had spent two more years in a school that was slowly killing her. Imagine if Brennan had stayed at a school where students called her racial epithets for daring to be smart.

This is how the nation denies genius. There are thousands of bright children who don't have access to the resources that these three children did and whose talents are being squandered in mind-numbing classrooms. Nurturing the nation's brightest minds shouldn't depend on luck. And it doesn't have to if we make a conscious decision to treat exceptional children as the exceptions they are. We need to realize that all children—even the brightest—have a right to an education appropriate to their abilities.

Chapter 2

The Sorry State of Gifted Education

For the Missouri Department of Elementary and Secondary Education to help fund a district's program for gifted students, "instructional sessions must be supplementary to the regular instructional program, both in content and in cost," the state's website says. Many other states and districts have the same policy. The classes that gifted students need most—accelerated math, English, and science—aren't supplementary; they're substitutes for the core curriculum, and therefore they are excluded from gifted programs.

So instead, in Missouri and other states across the country, many schools that want to do something for gifted students wind up offering them the equivalent of indoor camp.

A boy we know named Paul goes to one of these schools. Paul's university town is known for its good schools. The National Governors Association praised the town as a model district. A state review team recognized the town's gifted program as a "district strength." But even within this good gifted program in a good district, Paul's family soon learned how little gifted education in America does for highly intelligent kids.

Kindergarten work didn't challenge Paul, who could read far beyond grade level. His mother, June, asked if a grade skip would be appropriate. Paul's teacher said that wasn't wise for socialization reasons and because Paul's handwriting was a little slow. His math progress reports noted that he lacked "one-to-one correspondence." June thought this was odd, since Paul could add and subtract. The teacher explained, June says, that no child his age had that ability.

So Paul finished kindergarten. In first grade the school's accommodation for gifted students meant letting Paul and a few other children sit in the hallway for forty-five minutes a week doing word puzzles as kids tromped past them on the way to gym class or the bathroom. "He learned nothing his whole first grade year," June says. Not knowing what to do about his complaints, she had him tested. After much discussion about Paul's off-the-charts IQ scores, the school let him skip to third grade. There, he could be part of the official gifted program.

According to the program's brochure, Paul's district employs the "pull-out" method of gifted education, a common one in schools across the country that have a mandate and have appropriated funds to serve gifted children. Students go to special classrooms for ninety minutes to a few hours a week for enrichment—in general, studying noncurricular material such as mythology or building machines with Legos. A few pull-out programs across the country offer gifted students rigorous academic work and send them back to their regular classrooms with substitute math and reading assignments. But such programs remain rare. In Paul's district, "pull-out" meant that once a week all the third to fifth graders labeled as gifted would board the bus at their homeschools and travel to the Center for Gifted Education. The children would choose from enrichment topics deemed appropriate for their grade level. Paul was offered a choice between building a model city, learning about the legends of Robin Hood, or becoming "Bug Wise." He could not choose the aviation "Just Plane Fun" class offered to fourth and fifth graders or the class where students learned to use computers to illustrate their own books. Even in many gifted programs in this country, schools rely more on age than interest or ability to group children.

Gifted kids in general love their pull-out enrichment programs—camp is always more fun than school—although districts that offer these classes seldom explain why only gifted kids can learn about insects and Robin Hood, and why gifted kids can't learn algebra before eighth grade. Paul was happy enough to spend one fewer day per week in the regular classroom. Meanwhile, the other four school days each week made him more and more miserable. He knew all the third grade material already, so he wasn't learning—except how to live while being constantly bored. He returned, listless, to the family's farm in the afternoons. June considered moving to St. Louis so she could enroll him in a program for exceptionally gifted children there because the expert who tested Paul suggested that such a program would be a better fit.

She didn't want to break up her family, however, so she went to the district and asked what could be done. She accepted the administrators' assurances that her district would develop a program similar to the one in St. Louis. A special grant came through from Missouri state funds to hire a teacher. Paul's district planned to offer the program to a handful of elementary school students with IQs over 145.

Yet, somehow, Paul wound up being the only student accepted for the program, so the program was not implemented. The money went unspent, and Paul began fourth grade in a regular classroom. He kept going to the pull-out gifted program.

He grew increasingly frustrated with breezing through math assignments and reading books under the desk. Finally, just before the winter break, he informed his parents that he was quitting. He refused to go back to school, and no amount of persuasion or threats would change his mind. June tried homeschooling, but Paul grew restless in their isolated home. He liked being around other children. The only homeschooling support group June knew of in the area was affiliated with a church, and June was told that she would have to wait until August to join.

So Paul visited an independent (private) school at first, and then eventually the public school district found a teacher for the program for exceptionally gifted "student"—singular—Paul. The class would be held at the high school. In theory, Paul could have access to high school classes. Instead, he spent hours sitting in a windowless room in the high school's basement every day doing sixth grade worksheets to evaluate his level of advancement. He did this for the rest of the year while the part-time teacher graded her papers for another class. Paul's assessment was never finished. The transcripts for the distance-learning program he had done on his own through Stanford University's Education Program for Gifted Youth showed that he was ready for algebra, but he wasn't allowed near a high school math class. In the afternoons he went back to elementary school for classes with his age group. Yet the schedule wasn't coordinated: His regular class had already done the fun stuff like art and gym in the morning. He could take fourth grade math with them or else sit there for hour-long gaps and do nothing. June began to wonder if the school district was trying to make Paul so miserable that she'd start homeschooling again. As it was, she says, he had become a very depressed child.

The next year Paul finally decided he was tired of all the commotion in his short schooling history, and he was tired of being so different. He didn't like trying to learn all by himself. He asked to be in a normal fifth grade classroom. He'd learn to cope with being bored. He stopped going to the district's pull-out program. "The district said he was overqualified and would get nothing out of it," June says.

And so, in a good district that prides itself on its gifted program, this highly gifted child found the best option was to pretend he wasn't smart.

■ Education's Dirty Secret

Paul is one of hundreds of precocious young people from around the country whom we've met through our work with highly gifted children over the past few years. These children come from many different backgrounds and have many different strengths and needs, but all have intellectual abilities years beyond their chronological age. Four-year-olds read *Little House on the Prairie* books. Preteens revel in abstract mathematical reasoning. Middle schoolers write fantastical novels. High school students conduct scientific experiments solely to satisfy their own curiosity. All have minds capable of astonishing things. All of them need schools and teachers capable of challenging them to the extent of their abilities.

Yet, just like Paul's parents, many of the families we work with have discovered the dirty secret of gifted education in America. Gifted education is largely haphazard, ineffective, and underfunded; it is more style than substance and rarely provides what gifted kids truly need: work that challenges them to the extent of their abilities in an environment with other kids who love to learn.

Only twenty-nine states fund education programs for gifted students. Of these, many states offer Individual Education Plans (IEPs) for their gifted students, but in a large number of districts every "individual" plan says the same thing. Students may be offered "in-class enrichment," which depends on the teacher not being overwhelmed. One classroom study found that gifted students received the same assignments as the whole class in academic areas 84 percent of the time. Teachers most often individualized math assignments, but even then only 11 percent of gifted students' activities contained advanced materials. In-class enrichment may just mean giving gifted kids thirty math problems instead of fifteen. Other districts, such as Paul's, try to attract families by touting their gifted programs. However, these services tend to be pull-out enrichment programs where students study only noncurricular material. According to the 1993 National Excellence Report released by the U.S. Department of Education, more than 70 percent of elementary schools offering gifted programs are in this category.

Some school districts do not identify gifted children until the middle of elementary school, although highly gifted kids will strain at their constraints in kindergarten. A mother of one young boy we know discovered that instead of reminding her son to bring his lunch to school in first grade, she had to remind him to bring two books to read in the long hours after he finished each assignment and waited for the class to catch up. If he forgot his books, he'd have nothing to do. A gifted program that does not identify and serve students until third grade does nothing for a child like this.

Some school districts with gifted programs, or even schools for the gifted, fail to see any difference in levels of giftedness. One mother told us that she had an easier time getting a regular school to help her daughter than the school for the gifted she had been attending. The gifted school aimed to help moderately gifted children, and did, but refused to be flexible for children who still found the program unchallenging.

The problem continues past elementary school. Middle schools and high schools sometimes follow gifted education mandates by allowing bright students to work one grade level ahead in mathematics (algebra, for instance, in eighth grade) and to take honors English classes. But algebra doesn't help an eighth grader capable of calculus, and calling a class "honors" doesn't make it satisfy a gifted child's needs. We hear tales from gifted teenagers of high school honors English classes where the students must read and write book reports on novels they could comprehend in elementary school.

Private schools don't necessarily do any better. Betsy, mother of two of the children we've worked with, tells us that a school whose tuition was $10,000 per year per child instructed her second grader that it didn't matter if he could do complex math problems in his head. He still needed to complete all the grade-level worksheets with problems such as 8 + 7—and he needed to show his work. "All our children are gifted," the school told Betsy. It may have been true, but not all gifted children have the same intellectual ability. Betsy's son read David McCullough's thousand-page tome *Truman* in second grade. Programs designed to serve the second grader who is just figuring out chapter books will not help him.

None of these solutions truly serves the needs of highly gifted children, and many create their own problems. Pull-out programs that provide only enrichment, for instance, are elitist. All students would benefit from enrichment; you don't need to be gifted to put on a puppet show or learn the names of Greek gods. Who can blame other children for resenting that they are missing out on these programs? They merely satisfy a political need to do something to mollify parents of gifted children. And they don't provide what gifted children need, which is an advanced academic curriculum to match their abilities and the opportunity to explore topics in depth while surrounded by academic peers. Almost nowhere do bright children actually receive this kind of education program—a sorry state indeed.

■ Funding Priorities

There are no federal requirements for gifted education and almost no allocated federal funds. Consequently, gifted education exists only when states and school districts choose to offer and fund it. State budgets for gifted education vary widely, ranging from roughly $100 million a year to nothing.

Specific funding levels matter less than what states do with the money. But regardless, what strikes us, looking at these numbers, is how underfunded gifted education is compared to other educational services. "Special education," referring to the education of students with disabilities, represented more than 21 percent of the 1999–2000 spending on all elementary and secondary educational services in the United States. The fifty states and the District of Columbia spent roughly $50 billion that year on special education.

Clearly, a child with a severe physical disability will cost more to educate than other children, but when the number of children with disabilities and the number who could be labeled as at least moderately gifted both hover at around a tenth of the population each, why does special education receive twenty cents on the educational dollar while gifted education receives a fraction of a penny? Part of the answer is visceral: Disabled students clearly have needs, and what politician wants to ignore these

children? Society is compelled to help. But this generous funding is also a testament to the success of the special education
movement and what parents can achieve when they convince
legislators and the public at large that a problem needs to be
solved.

Until the last half-century or so, states frequently institution-
alized children with mental or physical disabilities, or excluded
them from educational services altogether by declaring them
"uneducable." Stories like that of Helen Keller, the blind and
deaf woman who graduated from Radcliffe in 1904 and achieved
much success as a writer and activist, are well known because at
the time few people thought disabled children could achieve
much at all.

Parents of disabled children understood the situation differently. The first parents advocacy groups gained clout in the
1930s and 1940s. Inspired by the civil rights movement and
the Constitution's equal-protection clause, they began calling in
the 1950s and 1960s for the states and the federal government
to ensure that children with disabilities received a free and appropriate education.

These activists found a sympathetic ear with President Lyn-
don Johnson's administration, which was already pushing
Great Society programs designed to bring previously marginal-
ized groups into the mainstream. A series of amendments in
the late 1960s to the Elementary and Secondary Education Act
of 1965 gave federal grants to state schools for the handicapped,
then to local districts, to promote the inclusion of students with
disabilities in local school communities.

Then, in 1975, Congress passed the Education for All Handicapped Children Act, known as Public Law 94-142. This landmark special education law mandated a free and appropriate
education for all children with disabilities in the "least restric-

tive environment," ensured due-process rights, mandated individual education plans, and provided funding to lessen the burden on the states.

Although the federal government never provided the 40 percent of special education funding it said it would, Congress does send billions of dollars a year to state programs for physically and mentally handicapped children. When President George W. Bush was pushing his 2003 education budget, the White House issued a press release detailing new special education funding for each state. The numbers are staggering: $319,826,974 for Pennsylvania; $295,771,312 for Michigan; $897,214,114 for California, and so on. The original PL 94-142 enjoys broad support. Regulations added since have expanded the scope of the original law to include, for instance, preschool children and those over eighteen. The core of the law was reauthorized in 1990 and again in 1997 as the Individuals with Disabilities Education Act (IDEA). Under the provisions of this law, many disabled children are in small classes with specially trained teachers capable of tailoring their lessons to each student's individual needs. Schools must provide any additional assistance—such as computer programs, tutoring, and so forth—that disabled children need to reach their potential.

But children with disabilities aren't the only ones who need special accommodations. All children should receive an education appropriate to their abilities—one that challenges them and helps them grow. This includes gifted children, too. Gifted children may not look different from other children, but they do have profound needs. Why should society neglect one group of special-needs children and support another?

Research shows that gifted students are at great risk for underachievement. Yet states and federal legislators, who have recently found it politically advantageous to mandate and fund services for children with disabilities, have been less inclined to remove the obstacles that keep gifted students from achieving their potential. Few choose to fund the programs and schools that the brightest children need to learn to the extent that they can.

Parents of gifted students do try to advocate for their children, and many rely on the model of the early special education movement. Some have been successful. Sympathetic legislatures have created state schools for gifted secondary students in North Carolina, Indiana, Illinois, and a few other states. In many states and school districts, however, gifted education is a luxury—something to be cut if the state or local budget needs trimming. Even Americans without gifted children of their own recognize the sorry state of affairs. A 1992 Gallup poll found that 61 percent of respondents felt schools should do more to educate and challenge their brightest students. And 84 percent said they would support "special funding for a program to provide a more challenging education for the smartest and most gifted children, as long as it did not reduce what was offered to average and slow learners." Yet attempts to capitalize on that support often run smack into a wall of indifference.

■ Too Expensive

Levi started school at age three, but he quickly found the work at his Los Angeles elementary school tedious. Levi's mother, Leila, enrolled him in a magnet gifted program. He was rapidly accelerated, and by age six was in fifth grade. But it still wasn't enough to satisfy his zeal for learning. He hated the school he was in and became very depressed. Eventually Leila tried to enroll him in classes at Santa Monica College, a community college in their neighborhood. But Santa Monica didn't want to take the boy because he lacked a high school diploma or equivalent and because the school had never had a student that young.

The battle to allow Levi to take California's high school equivalency exam and attend college turned Leila, an educator, into a full-fledged activist. The district didn't want him to take the exam. She tried calling her local representatives in the California assembly, but they didn't have much interest in the case. Eventually she found sympathetic ears in the Republican education caucus. She read the whole California education code and found eighteen areas that the caucus could address in the law to eliminate age discrimination in testing and college admission, among other things. She lobbied the school district—her old employer—for six months before they allowed her son to take the high school equivalency exam. Levi passed the test. Santa Monica College agreed that he could enroll if Leila attended all classes with him—a problem for a single mom with a full-time job. Eventually the college changed this rule to allow Leila to hire students or other responsible adults to chaperone Levi around campus.

After achieving some success with Levi, Leila decided to continue her activism to help other highly gifted students. She gained much attention for a recent effort: Assembly Bill 2626, which would have authorized school districts to include community college courses in highly gifted students' individual education plans. The bill also authorized kindergarten to twelfth grade governing boards to pay for these students' fees, tuition, instructional materials, and supplies, since the school district would still be able to collect the per-student payment for these children from the state. The California assembly passed A.B. 2626 unanimously, but Governor Gray Davis vetoed it in September 2002. "Given the State's current fiscal situation, I cannot sign this measure," he said; in short, it was too expensive.

It's debatable how much A.B. 2626 would have cost the state. California's annual revenue per student (funds raised from federal, state, and local sources) is $8,000. Santa Monica College charges California residents $11 per semester unit. But even if A.B. 2626 cost the state the $1 million Davis said it would, this sum should be compared with the nearly $900 million grant that President Bush's federal education budget proposed for special education in California and the $3 billion that California itself spends on meeting these children's needs. No wonder California assemblyman Jay La Suer, the bill's sponsor, deemed Davis's veto "a slap in the face" to California's highly gifted students. It amounts to telling highly gifted students that they are not worth pennies on the dollar given to educate children with other special needs.

As Leila discovered, changing laws takes years: from identifying the problem to finding sympathetic legislators, to writing legislation, to lobbying, to putting the issue to a vote, and trying again if the measure fails to pass. Lawsuits also take years to work through the courts. Any change brought through legislation or the courts will likely come too late for the family seeking it. Most parents know this, so they don't file suits or press for laws. "Families say, 'It's more important that I'm there at dinnertime' or 'It's more important that I help my child first,'" Leila says. It's easier to seek small accommodations for a child rather than grand changes in law and policy.

But this creates a cycle where nothing changes for gifted children, and many of them spend years in schools where, as one parent recounted, children stare at the floor because they find the dust patterns more interesting than the subject matter they've already learned. In addition, other parties have little interest in changing things, either. "Schools want to keep gifted kids exactly where they are—to keep up the test scores," Leila says. For instance, one family we know invested much time and effort in fighting a school's decree that their daughter miss several days of her accelerated math class to take a new grade-level standardized test that the state was thinking of using. The school wanted the girl's score reported in its average.

■ Three Weeks to Endure a Year

In the absence of good gifted programs and a commitment to individualized education in the vast majority of American schools, true learning for highly gifted kids has to be eked out from after-school or weekend programs, or during the summer. We often hear stories of children who live for three-week camps for gifted students at a few universities around the country.

Laura is one of those students. When she was twelve, her family moved from a district that offered ability-grouped academic classes with work two to three years above grade level to a district that did not. When she started seventh grade, her new school's authorities looked at her transcript that showed a completed algebra class, scratched their heads, gave her a second-year algebra book, and had her sit in the back of another math class to muddle through it. The teacher would check in but offered little guidance or instruction. Laura floundered and learned little the whole year, other than how it felt to be a curiosity in a corner by herself.

Her school did offer one concession to gifted students. Based on her 99th-percentile standardized test scores, she was permitted to participate in the Midwest Talent Search, a program of the Center for Talent Development (CTD) at Northwestern University. The talent search, similar to ones conducted by Duke and Johns Hopkins universities, identifies highly gifted children by giving them out-of-level tests. Laura took the SAT, a test normally taken by college-bound high school seniors. She scored a 660 on the math section, quite a bit above average for high schoolers. CTD sent her a catalogue of summer courses. She applied for a class in geometry.

Laura expected a challenging environment, but when she moved into her dorm on the Lake Michigan campus in July, she discovered a different world. Her geometry class, made up of students like her who had shown profound mathematical talent, met every day, exploring topics in depth and absorbing axioms as fast as the students could master them. The teacher helped students deduce each concept in the morning, then followed up with formulas and theorems in the afternoon. Laura was thrilled with her discoveries—the 1:2:3 ratio of empty space to spheres to cylinder in a tennis ball container, and the right angles in all triangles inscribed in a semicircle.

She also discovered a different world socially, where other students wanted to hear about her "aha!" moments. Since all of the summer program's students were highly gifted, they were no longer "nerds" or "geeks." In heady late-night discussions in her room, on weekend trips to Chicago, at dances, and during meals in the dorm cafeteria, she learned that other students might actually like her *because* of her intelligence, not *in spite* of it.

So Laura could hardly bear to leave after three weeks to go back to eighth grade at a school where most people seemed to wish they were elsewhere. For months Laura thought, "Three weeks ago at Northwestern I did this" or "Seven weeks ago at Northwestern I did that." She participated in the Midwest Talent Search again in January and, with her new geometrical knowledge, scored a perfect 800 on the math section of the SAT. She was glad because such a score meant she'd win a scholarship and could go back to Northwestern that summer. "Those three weeks let me endure the rest of the year," she says.

Laura's experience is common, says the Center for Talent Development's Paula Olszewski-Kubilius, who calls summer programs an "inoculation" against academic malaise during the rest of the year. In regular schools, she says, "gifted kids feel two things: First, an incredible lack of challenge in their classes. Second, they have a hard time being comfortable with themselves because no one else, they fear, will be comfortable with who they are." Her own daughter attended a CTD summer session and came away amazed that she could finally be herself and "didn't have to hide who she was."

Throw dozens of children like these together for a summer and the intellectual energy and thrill of finally being accepted practically lights the dorms.

Yet there's nothing magical about CTD's formula for helping gifted children thrive. "A lot of what we do can be replicated in schools if there's homogeneous grouping," Olszewski-Kubilius says. "Schools can replicate the level of challenge if they put kids together with other similarly motivated children."

But most don't. "There's a misconception that gifted kids will be okay anyway," Olszewski-Kubilius says. "Schools say, 'We have too many other kids to worry about.'"

That's a misguided notion. A child with SAT scores like Laura's is at risk for underachievement, just like the slower-learning children the standards movement was designed to help. Scores such as Laura's "mean the child is intellectually functioning at a college level—and college level for a pretty bright student," Olszewski-Kubilius says. "She's ready for coursework at the college level. She's ready for an accelerated course of instruction. She doesn't need to spend nine months doing algebra."

But chances are that in most American schools a student like Laura will spend every bit of that nine months doing work at most a year or two beyond grade level, and her school will still claim it educates the gifted.

Every year CTD, the Talent Identification Program at Duke, the Center for Talented Youth at Johns Hopkins, the Belin-Blank Center for Gifted Education and Talent Development at the University of Iowa, and a few scattered programs elsewhere provide thousands of bright children with a glimpse of what gifted education could be. Middle schoolers study geometry, as Laura did, or computer science, chemistry, or literature. In three weeks students learn more than they do in a whole year at their local schools. They discover the thrill of stretching their minds to the limit. They discover how wonderful it is to learn while surrounded by intellectual peers with similar drives to achieve.

Interestingly enough, many schools refuse to grant credit for these classes, claiming it's impossible to learn so much in such a short time. Credit will be granted, these schools say, not for learning material but for spending 180 days in a seat. In the current sorry state of gifted education, many bright students have to waste the whole year to be deemed sufficiently educated.

■ Isolated Bright Spots

While summer programs can be lifesavers, they can also be expensive. Northwestern's programs cost over $2,000 per student each session. And while CTD and other talent search programs make financial aid and scholarships available, many families aren't willing to endure the paperwork required or risk forfeiting their deposits if financial assistance isn't granted. So most of the young people at these summer camps come from upper- and middle-class families who can afford the tuition. This is why it's so important that equally satisfying school-based programs exist, particularly for children whose parents can't afford summer or weekend enrichment.

Some school districts have chosen to make these investments. Caryn Ellison, recently a runner-up for Indiana Teacher of the Year, teaches a self-contained gifted class in Mishawaka, Indiana. Mishawaka is a blue-collar town that is sustained by factories and retail-industry jobs. Its tiny houses, perched among gas stations along the St. Joseph River, don't generate the tax base of richer towns. Yet this community in northern Indiana has chosen to create academically advanced classes for its brightest young students. These students congregate in a magnet program at Twin Branch Elementary School where they can enroll in a first and second grade class, a third and fourth grade class, and Ellison's fifth and sixth grade class.

Ellison's energy charges the room. On a snowy November day she wakes up the class by asking in Spanish who needs lunch tickets—a simple way to force the children to think while doing rote activities. When kids give presentations on books they've read, they rate them universally as "ten out of ten"—less a sign of the books' quality than a testament to how much the students love to read. These kids rave about group projects; in previous classes, transplants to the Mishawaka program say, group projects meant they did most of the work. They like discussing their papers because they're sure their fellow students will have insightful comments. And they make friends who won't call them nerds.

Ellison notes that the children have varied abilities; some are very gifted while others are more moderately so. Some of her fifth graders read at a seventh grade level, and others at the level of high school seniors. Ellison, freed from simultaneously teaching children who can't read at all, can alter the curriculum for each child.

Still, she wonders what will happen to her students once they leave. A handful of children in the class, she says, are quite advanced in math. She gives them special work. Soon they will go to middle school, though, where the self-contained gifted program turns into the equivalent of honors classes, which at any school can have varying levels of difficulty. As seventh graders her students will likely enroll in pre-algebra even if they can work beyond that. But for two years she can keep these children happy, stretch their brains, and help them experience the joy of learning while being surrounded by their intellectual peers.

It costs no more to hire a few teachers for classes like Ellison's than to bus children somewhere for indoor camp–style enrichment once a week. It costs no more to concentrate the brightest students in one class than to have dozens of teachers instructing mixed-ability fifth grade classes throughout a district. These accelerated, self-contained classes do much more for gifted children than enrichment. Most pull-out programs provide little beyond a creative outlet—and since districts that offer such programs claim they are helping gifted children when they aren't, they are often worse than no programs at all.

Pull-out programs are, quite simply, political solutions. In recent years the dominant educational culture has shied away from grouping students by ability and changing the curriculum for gifted children. Most gifted programs satisfy a need to do something to attract parents to a district, but they do little to change the status quo and the militant devotion to so-called fairness that some activists have succeeded in spreading through school systems nationwide.

This is the state of gifted education today: Only a few more than half of the states require schools to provide any services. Those that do, often offer only in-class enrichment or pull-out programs that have gifted kids doing word puzzles and puppetry, not advanced academic work. Schools that do offer advanced academic work often refuse to accelerate more than a year or two, no matter how advanced the child may be. Attempts to change things are brushed off as too expensive or, in the case of Paul's family, twisted to make school so miserable that the child doesn't want to be gifted anymore. Yet educators and officials everywhere continue to insist that gifted kids will fend for themselves.

It's no wonder that about half of the families we work with homeschool. Others have moved or played "musical schools" to provide their children with an appropriate education. One mom complains, "I am struck by the notion that I am off *peddling* my children to various schools in the region, searching and pleading for an appropriate educational setting for them." In a country that valued intellectual ability, educators would be tripping over themselves to ensure that her children's time was well spent. "Instead," she says, "I waste tedious amounts of time searching, searching, searching for appropriate opportunities . . . time that should be spent in direct service to the kids. I can see why people throw in the towel and turn their backs on government schooling. I have wasted two and a half years trying to figure this all out without any help from the schools."

But not every family can homeschool. Paul's family tried, and it didn't work for them. Some parents lack the time; some students lack the temperament. States promise their citizens that they will provide an education to all children. It's a shame that parents have to homeschool because they feel they have no choice. And while we admire families who are willing to move to advance their children's education—one family we know quit their jobs to move from California to Colorado—not everyone's life is portable, and many families don't have the funds to pick up and start over. Siblings and other family members may be content where they are.

A nation that truly values achievement would do everything in its power to identify bright students wherever they happen to live and provide them with academic work that stretches their minds. A nation that truly values achievement would not spend billions on special education while allowing states to spend nothing on the gifted. And a nation that truly values achievement would not feel good about gifted-education classes based on Legos.

Instead, perhaps because of ignorance, but in many cases because of ideology, the nation prefers to live with the consequence of the sorry state of gifted education: thousands of frustrated kids whose talents are wasted. As the National Association for Gifted Children points out, "There is physical and psychological pain in being thwarted, discouraged, and diminished as a person. To have ability, to feel power you are never allowed to use, can become traumatic. Many researchers consider the gifted as the largest group of underachievers in education."

Chapter 3

The Lowest Common Denominator

I N 1954 ANTHROPOLOGIST Margaret Mead turned her atten-tion from the Samoans to investigate a different society: the American classroom. She was not impressed. "There is in America today an appalling waste of first-rate talents," she wrote. "Neither teachers, the parents of other children, nor the child's peers will tolerate the wunderkind."

This intolerance explains the sorry state of gifted education. It creates gifted students' twin torments: dumbed-down schools and an educational philosophy that demands that everyone do the same thing at the same time. These torments run as rampant now as they did when Mead wrote. If anything, they have grown worse.

This devotion to the lowest common denominator has no place in a country that needs the brainpower of its brightest citizens. Yet a complacent society has allowed anti-intellectualism and a false view of equality to waste students' time and talents and cause them considerable misery as well. Anti-intellectualism comes from misplaced priorities. Neglecting bright children so that slower children can catch up is done, appallingly enough,

in the name of "justice." Both deny gifted children the education they deserve. And both amount to a society shooting itself
in the foot.

■ Anti-intellectualism

Americans have always struggled with praising education but
being suspicious of those who learn too much. In the 1830s,
Alexis de Tocqueville warned that America's habit of glorifying
practical arts above theoretical reasoning could someday undermine the nation, as the "guiding light" of intellect would "dwin-
dle by degrees and expire of itself."

More than one hundred years later, the historian Richard
Hofstadter noted the same problem in *Anti-Intellectualism in
American Life,* his 1964 Pulitzer Prize–winning book about the
lack of deep thinking in business, politics, and education. As he
pointed out, America has a long history of practicality. Children
have always been taught that it is better to be good than wise.
Over time, people start to believe that good and wise don't mix
easily in the human soul.

That suspicion continues in a modern society so complex it
leaves people bewildered. President George W. Bush and former Vice President Al Gore played down their degrees from
Yale and Harvard, respectively, during the 2000 presidential
election. Television talk shows with their parade of miscreants,
magazines devoted to "news you can use," and vapid sitcoms do
little to engage the mind. Many books on the best-seller lists
read like greeting card fare. Cities burn money to build stadiums and lure sports teams while library hours are cut back to
the point where no one who holds a nine-to-five job can visit.
Athletic recruitment at the nation's top colleges dilutes their in-

tellectual character, crowding out philosophers and poets to make room for lacrosse and water polo teams. The growing preprofessionalism among young people means these same colleges flirt dangerously with paying more attention to grades and networking than to the pursuit of truth.

This practicality has pervaded America's primary and secondary schools from the beginning. When Thomas Jefferson proposed sending promising young boys from farms and the lower classes to college, one Virginia planter scoffed, "It is a great mistake to suppose that there is more knowledge or utility in philosophy than in the agricultural or mechanical arts. Take away the food of man and his existence would cease. Take away his philosophy and he would scarcely know it was gone." American society never has paid or valued teachers much. Throughout our history, many teachers chose their profession because they couldn't find work elsewhere or, in the case of women, were not allowed to use other talents. A chronic shortage of books in many schools meant, and still means, pupils memorized passages from outdated texts.

But these problems could be conquered in small schools devoted to academics. For much of the early history of the Republic, an army of bright, ambitious women taught pupils everything from reading to algebra to zoology. One-room schoolhouses couldn't last forever, though. As the population grew, and as immigrants filled American cities, education had to change. Enrollment in public schools rose from 7.6 million in 1870 to 12.7 million in 1890. New schools had to be built to accommodate these children.

This construction changed more than the number of pupils under one roof. It also changed the philosophy of education. The rise of large, common schools in the late 1800s and early 1900s meant a shift toward training students to live in a democratic, pluralistic society rather than just training young minds. Horace Mann and the other fathers of public, compulsory schooling championed education for everyone. Universal education is still one of America's noblest ideas. The original idea of sending all children to school in order to find and nurture talent from all walks of life, however, has yet to be achieved.

As millions of previously underserved children poured into American schools, educators decided to make school a great equalizer. Unable to fathom teaching immigrant children Latin and trigonometry, educators decided to dismiss much of the classical curriculum as irrelevant. In the National Education Association's "Cardinal Principles of Secondary Education," devised in 1918 at the height of the Progressive era, the curriculum committee wrote that schools placed too much emphasis on the intensive pursuit of academic subjects. Instead, the commission called for the curriculum to include agricultural, business, clerical, industrial, and other studies. "Provision should be made also for those having distinctively academic needs," the commission wrote, as if academics were merely an afterthought.

In that anti-intellectual environment, John Dewey's *Democracy and Education* (published in 1916) excited those who liked the idea of escaping the traditional curriculum with its pesky standards and difficult goals. While Dewey himself remained concerned with the pursuit of truth by unconventional means, those who invoked his name decided that a democratic education meant dispensing with Shakespeare to learn about traffic safety.

Then, in the 1950s and 1960s, the "life adjustment" phase of education geared school toward children who would not go on to college or skilled trades, and even college-bound students were steered toward nonacademic work. Hofstadter cites, for example, a report by President A. Whitney Griswold of Yale that an otherwise promising young man from the Midwest had applied to Yale but could not be admitted because the bulk of his last two years of high school consisted of chorus, speech, typing, physical education, Marriage and Family, and Personality Problems classes.

Standards movements—first in the wake of *Sputnik* in 1957 and then, in response to the 1983 Department of Education report, "A Nation at Risk"—beefed up the curriculum, but these crusades, too, ultimately focused on low achievers. Consider the current devotion to standardized tests under the No Child Left Behind Act of 2001. Being drilled on grammar and arithmetic may help slower children learn basics and is certainly an improvement on schools that, gripped by what President Bush called the "soft bigotry of low expectations," failed in the past even to do that. But such rote learning does nothing to engage a bright child's intellect. "A Nation at Risk" warned that schools weren't challenging their gifted students. But as we saw in the last chapter, gifted programs put in place since have done little to ease the dulling of America's brightest minds.

The results show that American students continue to lag behind students in other industrialized nations, and the brightest learn to coast through school, seldom stretching their brains. A young woman we know named Maya, for instance, received high grades at her midwestern high school, which was considered the best in its district. Her classmates elected her student council president, and she became an editor of the student newspaper. She was miserable the whole time. "High school was all about fitting in," she says, "and I never fit in." She never studied more than two hours for a test. She slid through the toughest classes in her school. Her ninth grade honors biology teacher had the class sing songs and just sit and read the text-book. In another science class a teacher told her to change her lab results to fit what his handbook said she should have seen. When she protested that this wasn't part of the scientific method, he docked her grade. She survived high school, she says, by telling herself that she was "going to a better place." But even applying to college made her crash into her school's apathy. The whole school had two guidance counselors, neither of whom was thrilled about filling out the paperwork for any school but the state university. "They told me not to apply to so many schools," Maya says. But she did. She got into Harvard. She arrived in Cambridge, Massachusetts, with no idea how to study. She didn't know how to write papers. She didn't even know what a thesis was. She floundered her whole freshman year, shocked by the tragedy of wasted time that her sleepwalk through primary and secondary schooling had been.

Like Maya, the brightest students in America waste most of their time in school. They read books aimed years below their capabilities and write five-paragraph essays on trees. They goof off in math lectures, confident that they'll be able to race through their homework in five minutes on the bus. They adhere to a rigid social system where the content of their character matters less than the cut of their jeans. They note who sits next to whom at lunch, pass notes, scheme their way onto the cheerleading squad or football team—or worship those who do. High schools—and many middle schools, too—have become cults reminiscent of *Grease* and *Clueless*, ongoing pep rallies likely to drive the intellectually curious mad. Other elements of school, such as having a locker, eating in a cafeteria, or riding a bus, aren't crucial to education, either, but the education establishment has succeeded in convincing people that they are. Whenever we mention kids going to college early, someone asks, "But what about the prom?" as though gifted young people should suffer four years of boredom for one magical night.

Schools are happy to have highly gifted students for two weeks at the end of senior year when they can announce, as Maya's school did, that they send students to Harvard. They pat themselves on the back for having produced such stars. The rest of the time, anti-intellectualism runs rampant and bright students are on their own.

■ Two Views of Equality

This dumbing down is only part of the problem. Schools also reach the lowest common denominator by preaching about one kind of "equality" to the exclusion of excellence. Equality sounds very nice and American, enshrined as a self-evident truth in the Declaration of Independence. Unfortunately, "equality" doesn't mean the same thing to everyone. To us, "equality" means equal opportunity to excel according to one's talents.

Too often, America fails to live up to this promise of equal educational opportunity. Schools in less privileged districts often face obstacles that can make learning a miracle when it happens. Cramped, dingy conditions can put anyone in a foul mood. Competent, experienced teachers have their choice of schools, so they don't choose schools in unsafe neighborhoods. Principals in these schools face such staffing shortages that they often must hire anyone who walks in with a license, and they still rely on long-term substitutes who have no stake in the achievement of these kids. Children from poor or troubled homes need school to be a haven, yet schools that ration books with missing covers and pages send a message to children that they are not worth good copies. Schools infested with rats or cockroaches tell children that they are not worth the cost of keeping a building clean.

And worse than these problems are the chronically low expectations that too many adults hold for children who don't come from middle-class homes. When college isn't expected, fewer students go to college. When schools don't offer rigorous classes or demand high-level work, children do not learn to the extent of their abilities. Schools that don't offer music, drama, or art won't find exceptional talent among students whose parents can't afford instruction. Budding mathematicians will not surge forward in schools where most of the math teachers aren't fully competent in the subject themselves, nor will scientists emerge from schools with so little lab equipment that students have to make do with whatever substitutes for beakers and Bunsen burners they can find.

All children in schools where solving disciplinary problems or merely avoiding chaos is more important than learning, suffer from diminished instruction. The brightest suffer most, because they experience the greatest gap between their talents and their opportunities. That their education limits them rather than helps them soar is a national shame. Schools should function so that all children can rise according to their ambition, perseverance, and intelligence—regardless of race, religion, or social status. This is what we mean by "equality."

But there's another kind of "equality" people talk about—one that doesn't mean equal opportunity. Some people believe that in democratic institutions such as schools, children should have not just equal opportunities to excel, but the same experiences and, as much as possible, equal outcomes. They should be taught the exact same material at the same time. If this bores the brightest, so be it. The social goals of schooling are more important than any child's educational aspirations. Children should stay with their age peers, these people believe. Grouping children by ability contradicts some fundamental notion of "fairness." And even if specialized schools for high-ability students take nothing from other public schools, they provide a different, selective environment and so are automatically suspect. "The sorting of students into groups . . . contradicts American values of schools as democratic communities of learners which offer equal educational opportunity to all," writes Anne Wheelock, author of *Crossing the Tracks: How "Untracking" Can Save America's Schools.*

Those who hold such a philosophy of one-size-fits-all education call themselves "egalitarians," but it's a strange, radical kind of egalitarianism, the kind that willingly sacrifices gifted kids to their view of fairness. Bright kids pay a very high intellectual price when they are kept in regular classrooms and are not given accelerated classes with their intellectual peers. That doesn't matter to these false egalitarians. If not all students can achieve at high levels, these critics of gifted education believe, then it is better that no one does. Such a philosophy is puzzling. With few exceptions, society doesn't work this way. Sports teams hire the best pitchers or point guards they can afford. Successful companies promote their most valuable and productive employees.

Yet this other kind of equality—based on false stereotypes of gifted kids, ignorance of their needs, and hostility toward those whose intelligence challenges the status quo—runs rampant in education today. This false notion of equality translates into schools informing parents that "all our children are gifted" and then refusing to challenge the brightest because such nurturing would smack of elitism. It means squandering childhoods in the name of the bad idea that leveling is more important than excellence.

■ Leveling

This false egalitarianism takes many forms. A mother we know tells the story of her neighbor, the local school superintendent, paying a visit. He mentioned that his own children had been identified as gifted, but he took them out of the school's gifted program because he felt that, as head of the town's schools, he shouldn't appear elitist. Not wanting their children to think they were smarter than other kids, he and his wife decided they could provide enrichment for them at home. Then they never got around to it, finding it more tolerable to thwart their children's education than change their mind-set.

This same mind-set shows up in political action against gifted education. New York City, for instance, is home to three public "exam schools"—Stuyvesant, Brooklyn Tech, and Bronx Science—which enroll gifted secondary students based on their performance on the Specialized Science High School Admission Test. Students are drawn from every community of New York's melting pot; many of them are children of immigrants. In the city's sea of public school mediocrity, these schools offer students a free elite education. But because of the selective nature of these schools, they have drawn protests from groups such as the Association of Community Organizations for Reform Now (ACORN), which charges that the exams are biased and the city's efforts to provide pretest tutoring for poor and minority students are inadequate. In 1997, ACORN issued a report demanding that the New York school board "suspend the competitive testing for the specialized high schools." It also claimed that these premier schools are "glaring symbols of what is wrong with our public schools," even though these exam schools enroll hundreds of black and

Hispanic youngsters. ACORN even held a protest in the Stuyvesant school lobby.

This same activist group also undertook a study of New York City's schools in 1996 that found, disturbingly, black and Hispanic parents received less information from schools on gifted programs than white parents. Yet rather than demanding fairer policies so that talented minority children would have access to these programs, ACORN announced: "We call for an immediate moratorium on all so-called gifted programming for grades K through 3."

This leveling also shows up when educators deny that differences in intelligence exist with the claim that "there are not really gifted children, just kids whom parents have pushed and spent time prepping." Or they say, "all children even out by third grade," though clearly they don't.

One principal we know removed books from a kindergarten classroom because he became alarmed that some children showed up at school already knowing how to read them. He felt that all the children should learn to read together.

Elizabeth's parents learned that their daughter would not be allowed to do fifth grade math in fourth grade—"then what would she do in fifth grade?" After they insisted on (and paid for and installed) software on the classroom's computer so she could study on her own, the school relented. But then Elizabeth learned that, having done fifth grade math, the school honestly meant she would have nothing to do in fifth grade. She could read some history books instead, the teacher said. That way she'd be in the same place as the other fifth graders by the end of the year.

Leveling shows up when educators decide that "in-class enrichment" can mean asking highly gifted students to tutor the other children in class when the gifted students have finished their assignments. A surprising number of educators believe that teaching others helps children learn better. It does—if both children are relatively unfamiliar with the topic. But how much better can a child learn a topic he has mastered? Making bright kids tutor others denies them the opportunity to learn to the extent of their abilities and holds them back with the rest of the class. But, again, this is exactly what the levelers want to do.

Anna's elementary school teachers told her she was moving too fast, so they tried to slow her down by requiring her to color worksheets in addition to completing them.

Leveling means teachers assigning "cooperative learning projects" that pair students of vastly different abilities. One education writer says that teachers should "have students work together in small groups on a task toward a group goal—a single product (a set of answers, a project, a report, a piece or collection of creative writing, etc.) or achieving as high a group average as possible on a test—and then reward the entire group on the basis of the quality or quantity of its product." Any experienced teacher knows this practice leads to bright and motivated students doing all the work, or at least getting much less out of the experience. Paula's eighth grade English teacher partnered her with students who risked failing. Paula's feedback improved their papers. Whether these students' feedback improved Paula's writing did not figure in the equation.

Phony egalitarians also resist the idea of separating children at all, preferring "full-inclusion classrooms," which rarely meet top students' needs. Says one parent who lobbied fruitlessly for gifted education: "The general consensus was that the school did not separate out the bright kids because it would be politically disastrous to suggest that some kids were 'smarter' than others."

In the face of resistance, many districts don't bother. Catherine's search for a job in academia took her to six different states as she tried to choose a school system or an independent school that would accommodate her highly gifted son. She talked with people from all six areas. None of these schools in university towns felt they had any obligation to help provide an appropriate education.

Phony egalitarianism shows up in budget debates. Lucy's district had a good gifted program, but targeted cuts slimmed it considerably. The PTA pledged to provide money for enrichment activities but then turned down a teacher who requested funds for an academic contest because such a competition would appeal only to the smart kids.

Jay's parents met with his principal after realizing their son wasn't being challenged. The principal insisted that other children who weren't complaining were just as bright as Jay. He proved it by showing them other children's test scores (with the names blacked out), which indicated that they, too, had scored at the 99th percentile on grade-level tests. Jay's parents tried to explain the ceiling effect of grade-level tests—that out-of-level tests used in talent searches show as much variance in the top percentiles as over the rest of the grade-level bell curve—but the principal would have none of it.

Leveling even shows up in ridiculous statements, like one administrator's explanation for why a mathematically precocious eight-year-old couldn't take classes with adolescent children: "The girls will all be getting their periods this year," the administrator said. *They will?* Her incredulous mother asked. *In math class?* A teacher strongly advised another of the families we work with not to accelerate their daughter because then she wouldn't develop breasts at the same time as the other girls.

These educators found it easier to make the sexist assumption that a girl's physical development trumps her mental development than question their devotion to everyone of the same age doing the same thing at the same time.

■ Training Teachers

These statements and decisions by teachers and administrators aren't made in a vacuum. They are made because schools don't make nurturing bright students a priority. They are made because spending public money on low achievers feels charitable, but investing in high achievers doesn't induce the same self-righteousness. They are made because of the unquestioned doctrine that children should march in lockstep through school and be grouped by age, not ability.

We don't mean to imply that all educators believe in catering to the lowest common denominator. We know teachers and principals who have tried hard to help gifted children succeed. We know teachers who have gladly made accommodations for gifted children once they were presented with research supporting these measures and others who pushed for these accommodations on their own.

So we agree with Susan Assouline of the University of Iowa's Belin-Blank Center for Gifted Education and Talent Development, who says of the average classroom teacher, "I don't believe it's open hostility. It's a combination of ignorance and complacency, that 'what we're doing is good enough.'" Most teachers want to do the best job possible for all their students. Reality simply lulls people into indifference. When teachers have limited time, differentiating the curriculum becomes a burden. Since gifted kids usually don't fail classes, a seventh grader who can't read becomes a bigger classroom crisis than a seventh grader whose mind is shutting down from learning fractions again. Faced with increased pressure to ensure the school and district that every child will pass the state's standardized test, teachers figure that a child scoring at the 99th percentile needs nothing more.

We blame this attitude on teachers' colleges and state regulations regarding teacher training that do not make gifted education a priority. Gifted education faces two obstacles with teacher training. First, since most gifted children remain in regular classrooms, all teaching candidates should be trained in gifted education, just as prospective teachers learn about reaching other populations. Yet most teaching programs offer little exposure to the needs of bright students; many don't even offer courses in gifted education. Second, because we hope that one day all districts will have classrooms and schools for the gifted (since research shows gifted children best achieve their potential in these environments), America needs a critical mass of teachers specifically certified in gifted education. Yet many major teaching schools don't offer concentrations in gifted education, and only half of the states offer certification in this area.

The most recent "State of the States" report published by the National Association for Gifted Children (NAGC) found that in the majority of states (67%), less than 10% of the teachers had training in teaching gifted students. Of the largest schools of education in the country that responded to our queries, none required any courses on gifted learners; few even offered them. Minnesota State University at Mankato, a top ten teacher's license–producing school, offers one elective class on gifted education at the undergraduate level. Indiana State University reports that nothing on gifted education is available for undergraduates. Northern Arizona University offers a certificate in gifted education for those who are interested, but those headed for regular classrooms will not encounter much information on gifted learners. Neither will those at the other large schools of education in the country, including the California state universities at Northridge and Fresno, and Eastern Michigan University.

Regular classroom teachers aren't the only ones in the dark. Teachers of gifted classes also receive little training for these positions. A 2003 survey found that twenty-nine states offer certification or endorsement in gifted education, and in four of these states that certification is optional. In the other twenty-one states, teachers of gifted classes need no particular expertise.

These states assume that a good teacher can teach anyone. Certainly, a good teacher can do amazing things. However, even the most talented music instructor would be less effective at teaching the trumpet if her training consisted of teaching the clarinet. Likewise, a brilliant teacher who specializes in teaching early–elementary school children to read will be less effective in developing the critical reading skills of a seven-year-old who already reads at an adult level. A *Gifted Child Quarterly* study a few years ago found that teachers of the gifted with three to five graduate courses in gifted education were significantly more effective in instruction, and in creating a positive classroom environment, than teachers with no specialized coursework.

Yet a teaching candidate pursuing those three to five courses would have a hard time finding them in many schools of education. Only twenty-nine states (of the forty-five responding to NAGC's survey) reported an undergraduate endorsement (or specialization) in gifted education. Of the large teaching schools just mentioned, Northern Arizona University and Minnesota State University at Mankato, offer graduate credentials in gifted education, but the California state universities and Eastern Michigan University do not.

The National Board for Professional Teaching Standards (NBPTS) offers a National Board Certification for which master teachers prove their excellence through portfolios of student work and videotaped sessions. NBPTS offers this widely sought credential in twenty-four areas, including Early Adolescence Through Young Adulthood/Career and Technical Education, but not gifted education.

Academia is also prone to fads, and teachers' colleges are no exception. In many schools, prospective teachers learn more about self-esteem and flashy ideologies than how to promote academic achievement. Gifted education isn't trendy. The Stanford University School of Education lists dozens of faculty interest areas, from feminism to sociocultural theory, but gifted education is not among them. Calling ideas "social constructs" is another hot academic topic. James Borland, a Columbia Teachers College professor of gifted education, published a paper recently calling giftedness itself a "social construct." By the time this paper, called "The Death of Giftedness," winds through the work of various philosophers, Borland reaches the same conclusion that most of us already have: namely that pull-out programs for gifted students don't do any good. Unfortunately, "Giftedness Education Expert Says Giftedness Is Just Social Construct" is the message being broadcast.

■ The War on Genius: Ability Grouping

But ignorance, complacency, and trendiness are only part of the problem. While the average classroom teacher is simply trying to juggle the competing demands of different students while working for too little money in a job rarely held in high esteem, more ideological educators, academics, and politicians want to impose their leveling agenda on schools. They see schools as places more for social engineering than learning, and so they seek to undermine what accommodations for bright children do exist and derail attempts at new ones.

Schools are ripe for utopian schemes. On any given weekday, 90 percent of America's children sit in public school classrooms ready to absorb whatever ideology or social cause dreamers want to impart along with reading, writing, and arithmetic. Some of these causes have been quite noble. Children in schools learn tolerance for other religions and cultures, and they learn the civic responsibilities necessary for living in a democratic society. In the early twentieth century, educators threw themselves into the task of making immigrants into good Americans. In the 1950s and 1960s the desegregation movement sought to bring children of all colors into classrooms together, sure that if they learned together, they could learn to live together. While those wedded to the bigoted ways of the past fought bitterly to preserve whites-only schools, in many places around the country desegregation actually succeeded and provided more equal educational opportunities to those who had previously been stuck in the inferior schools reserved for minority children. In these desegregated schools, many minority or otherwise underserved children achieved as much as the brightest white and more privileged children. Others, unfortunately, did not. Plenty of well-to-do children also failed to learn as quickly as some of their classmates.

At first idealistic educators thought such change would just take time. But when equal outcomes continued to prove elusive, some chose to believe that the fault lay in how schools grouped students for instruction, not in children's different abilities.

And so in the name of faulty research and the ideology of fairness, schools and districts across the country have shied away from giving high-ability students accelerated instruction with their intellectual peers—at a very high cost to these students' futures.

When schools group children according to test scores or knowledge of subject material, or create self-contained classes or schools for gifted children, this is called "ability grouping" or "homogeneous grouping." Some people call this practice "tracking," though that term refers more to the high school habit of separating students into vocational, regular, and college preparatory classes. Most schools practice at least some form of ability grouping, such as reading groups or honors math classes, but few schools group extensively, particularly in the primary grades, or do so very effectively.

Ability grouping, like all educational practices, can be done right or done wrong, and wrong is often easier than right. All children deserve to learn and all children deserve high standards, but as detracking crusader Jeannie Oakes points out in *Keeping Track: How Schools Structure Inequality,* remedial classes are plagued by chronically low expectations. For instance, many remedial high school English classes don't study or attend performances of Shakespeare, although the Bard wrote his plays for the illiterate Elizabethan masses. And in an era where more and more jobs require higher education, too many basic-level classes do not help students develop the higher-level thinking and problem-solving skills necessary to pursue college. Schools with inflexible tracks that give students and parents little say over course selection are particularly galling, especially for students who may not be identified as bright because of race, social class, or conduct. And sometimes schools group students fairly but then give every class the same curriculum regardless of students' ability to comprehend it. Clearly, this pseudo-grouping accomplishes nothing.

But rather than urge reforms of these problems, critics cite two main objections to the idea of grouping itself: first, that research shows "the brightest and highest achieving students appear to do well regardless of the configuration of the groups they learn with," as Jeannie Oakes writes, and second, that students consigned to lower tracks learn less than they could in mixed settings and feel worse about themselves as well.

Because of these and other objections, "ability grouping" has become a dirty phrase in many education circles these days. Following a spate of books such as Oakes's in the 1980s, sympathetic groups from the National Association of School Psychologists to the National Council of Teachers of English (NCTE) leaped onboard the anti-grouping wagon. "Segregation of students based upon the perception of ability denies equity in education by denying students the right to participate in the richest language environment possible," NCTE says. Some attorneys have called detracking the new civil rights issue. Judges have urged detracking as part of desegregation settlements. In 1994, for instance, the San Jose Unified School District agreed to detrack students in grades kindergarten to nine, and partially detrack grades ten to twelve (the consent decree has since been modified). And while we know of no schools or districts that have completely abolished ability grouping, the overall education climate leads many schools to believe that they better serve the cause of equity by insisting that all curricular changes for gifted students occur within the regular classroom.

Yet for all their influence, the critics of ability grouping are just plain wrong on the research. High-ability students may do well in any class configuration, but the highly gifted students we know would continue to score at the 99th percentile on standardized tests whether they attended class or not. Doing well does not mean doing one's best.

When James Kulik, director of the Office of Evaluations and Examinations at the University of Michigan, reviewed twenty-three major studies on grouping, he found that when high-ability students were placed in enriched classes, they gained four or five months academically on high-ability students who were left in regular classes. When gifted students received accelerated classes, they advanced as much as a whole year compared to students of similar age and intelligence. In other words, for every year a highly gifted child is left in a regular, unenriched classroom, she loses a year of what her intellectual capabilities in that subject could have been. This is a very high price to pay in the name of equity.

But what makes opposition to grouping even sadder is that the critics aren't correct regarding what happens to slower learners, either. Kulik's analysis found that specific subject grouping (such as reading groups separated by level) helps slower students learn more, particularly if students are grouped across grades, which is done in the widely used Success for All program. Studies of this grouping practice have shown that low-achieving fourth graders gained as much as two-thirds of an academic year over control groups of similar students in mixed-ability classes.

As for the issue of self-confidence, despite Oakes's fretting that students in lower level classes think "school's all right, but I'm not so good," slower students actually show a slight rise in self-esteem in ability-grouped classes. Researchers have found that children develop a self-concept by comparing themselves to others around them. Ability grouping can even shake high achievers' self-assurance. As new students at selective high schools such as Stuyvesant in New York City will tell you, they learn the first day that they aren't the smartest kids in the world.

Critics claim that ability grouping hurts slower students because teachers spend more time actually teaching in high-track classes, but studies show the difference is only a percentage point or two of class time. If that extra minute stems from discipline problems, as it usually does, placing these children in mixed-ability classes won't make the time off task disappear. Furthermore, recent studies of schools that tried to do away with ability grouping found that detracking brings no guarantee of high-quality instruction for everyone and will quite likely impose a lower equality on all students. Leveling down is easier than leveling up. Instead of all classes requiring higher-level, abstract thinking, no classes require it. Only the most stubborn opponent of ability grouping would see that as an improvement.

■ The War on Genius: Race, Class, and the Myth of Social Privilege

Even if levelers can't justify the abolition or absence of advanced classes or schools for the gifted because of educational efficacy, there is another card up their sleeves. Schools prepare students to live in a pluralistic society, they say, and so grouping by ability is by nature wrong. Unfortunately, in many gifted programs or other high-ability classes, some minority children are underrepresented compared to their percentage in the area population. And since children from better educated families tend to show higher IQs than children from impoverished ones, critics claim that ability grouping simply widens the gap between the haves and have-nots. As Mara Sapon-Shevin says in her book *Playing*

Favorites: Gifted Education and the Disruption of Community,
"These programs speak to us of unequal educational opportunities, racism, elitism, and exclusion." Programs for the gifted
mean that "we believe rich children deserve a better education
than poor children," she says, and are only for "the kids with
disposable income."

Talk of giftedness or intelligence often comes around to
these complicated subjects of race and class. As the mid-1990s
furor over Charles Murray and Richard Herrnstein's *The Bell
Curve* showed, America's discomfort with these issues lurks
very close to the surface. Some critics of gifted education charge
that any discussion of intelligence just means using code words
for race and socioeconomic status.

It is true that in gifted programs where entrance is based on
tested IQ, blacks and Hispanics are underrepresented compared
to their population within the district or school. Critics charge
that even if schools and districts don't harbor any particular prej-
udice, these statistics show discrimination either within the tests
themselves or in the concept of intelligence. (These same critics
are often silent on the case of another minority group, Asians,
who tend to be overrepresented, often several times over.)

We can't explain the differences in representation. We do
know, as fifty-two leading experts in the field of intelligence out-
lined in a 1997 *Wall Street Journal* editorial entitled "Mainstream Science on Intelligence," that intelligence denotes the
"ability to reason, plan, solve problems, think abstractly, comprehend complex ideas, learn quickly, and learn from experience. It is not merely book learning, a narrow academic skill, or
test-taking smarts." These researchers wrote that intelligence
can be measured and that IQ tests measure it well. "They are
among the most accurate (in technical terms, reliable and valid)
of all psychological tests and assessments," they said. The ex-

perts also stated that "intelligence tests are not culturally biased against blacks or other native-born English-speaking peoples in the U.S. IQ scores predict equally accurately for all such Americans, regardless of race and social class." Indeed, people of all ideological stripes are willing to use IQ tests to identify students for special education. It's only high IQs used for educational purposes that make people wary.

We don't know what part of intelligence is due to nature or nurture. We do know that children who grow up in homes without books and homes in which adults rarely speak to and interact with children will likely perform lower on IQ tests than children from more stimulating environments. We know that some cultures value intellectual ability in children more than others. Nothing alarms us more than hearing from gifted African American children we've met that classmates accuse them of "acting white" for their achievements. We help children from blue-collar families learn that working with one's mind is as valuable and honest as working with one's hands.

We also know that a feverish, insatiable intellect can arise in any situation. Genius does not discriminate. If parents can't or won't nurture that intelligence, it's doubly important that the community and schools do so.

For our work at the Davidson Institute for Talent Development, we have a simple policy on race: We don't ask. We do, however, get to meet these children and young people once they become involved in our programs. And inevitably, when we look around at the gatherings we sponsor, we see profoundly gifted kids of all colors and socioeconomic levels. Parents fret about how to make ends meet if Mom quits her job to homeschool. Single parents worry about how they can find the time to meet their children's needs. Immigrant families struggle to find ways to help their children grow while finding their own place in

America, often without the "disposable income" Sapon-Shevin writes about.

We are always surprised when people think that highly gifted kids come only in white and upper-class flavors. This false assumption fuels many of the misguided policies that experts in education, social sciences, and public policy have touted to prove their enlightenment. They claim we are all equal—not just before the law or God, but in actual ability or potential. They claim that all children are gifted, possessing one of "multiple intelligences," from knowing how to dance to knowing themselves, and we just have to discover where those equally valuable gifts lie. They dismiss talk of intelligence or IQ as simply a social construct, and resist attempts to structure education around this concept, deeming it undemocratic and probably racist and classist, too.

People are certainly entitled to their beliefs, but we cannot let them claim that they are advancing the cause of justice in America. Foisting "equality" to the exclusion of excellence on schools hurts bright children, but it does not hurt all bright children equally. Rich parents of highly intelligent children can afford tutors or summer classes or enrichment opportunities; they can afford to move to other districts or pay tuition for a private school more amenable to challenging work; they can forgo one parent's income so the child can be homeschooled if a school district refuses to offer an appropriate education. Poor families are simply stuck with the schools and districts they get. Is the cause of equity advanced by failing to help these children?

The levelers never seem to ask this question. Instead, they let an obsession with exact population parity lead to calls for an end to gifted programs that high-achieving poor and minority children need most. Jonathan Kozol, author of *Savage Inequalities: Children in America's Schools*, sympathetically quotes a New York

City resident's observation that academically selective schools such as Bronx Science and Stuyvesant constitute a "citywide skimming policy." Creating magnet schools in cities such as Washington, D.C., "is a loser's strategy," Kozol himself says. "Favor the most fortunate among us or they'll leave us too. Then we will have even fewer neighbors who can win political attention for our children." In other words, these false egalitarians believe gifted urban children should be held hostage to others' political needs.

While we agree that many poor and urban schools exist in states of deplorable disrepair and underachievement, nurturing the brightest is far from a "loser's strategy." Yes, all schools need higher standards; when elementary schools don't teach kids to read and when high schools graduate students without the skills necessary to pursue most jobs or college, we have a scandal. But the creation of good schools shouldn't require forcing bright students to remain in these bad schools until their parents or the children themselves revolt. A childhood can't be repeated; squandering a bright mind in the name of a future utopia is hardly justice.

In an ideal world, cities would keep their gifted magnet programs and raise standards at all schools. But until we have an education system whose resources are not severely limited, choices must be made. To counter small-minded stereotypes about the race and class of gifted students, all children should be evaluated early to find the brightest. Then school systems should pledge to make nurturing these children's talents a priority. Unlike the levelers, we think bright children deserve the best that the country has to offer. After all, they're most likely to pay that investment back many times over. They don't deserve to be abandoned to boredom and underachievement to satisfy someone else's agenda.

Chapter 4

Parenting Pushy Kids

D ESPITE THE SORRY state of gifted education in America and the forces pushing gifted students toward the lowest common denominator, some gifted children do have successful schooling experiences and childhoods that are not marred by an appalling waste of time and talent. These children tend to have parents who realize that their sons and daughters are exceptional, and like other exceptional children, these young people have special needs. These parents realize that nurturing intellectual development in their inquisitive, precocious, and pushy kids is an ongoing process that begins at home and can't just be delegated to schools.

Jane knew her son, Eric, was bright, but she didn't know how bright. He was an only child, and since the family lived in an isolated part of Maine, she knew few other children to compare him with. Eric always loved language. He looked at books and learned to speak at a very young age. He needed constant entertainment, and he couldn't sit still in his high chair. When he was two, he started noticing small words. When Jane drove past a gas station, he would call from his car seat, "Momma, what does g-a-s spell?" He saw the bright red octagons at the corner and asked the meaning of s-t-o-p. Then, three months before his third birthday, as they drove past a shopping center, he called out "Momma, that sign says 'paperback!'" Jane backed up the car and asked where. He pointed to a store's marquee, and sure enough, that's what it said. Eric had taught himself how to read.

After that he devoured words wherever he could find them. Jane attended a conference on gifted education and mentioned that her son, at age four, was reading the newspaper. One educator insisted that he be tested, and Jane agreed. Eric scored off the charts. When it came time for him to enroll in school, she met with the local elementary school principal and showed him her information on Eric. The principal said Eric seemed like a very bright little boy, and the school would look forward to having him in class.

Then Jane's husband lost his job, and the family had to move. They landed in Bangor, Maine. The school there told Jane they had no legal obligation to help her gifted son, and he would have to attend class with other kids his age. So Eric wound up in a regular classroom. He chafed at the environment. He argued with the teacher. He grew frustrated with the other children, who couldn't learn as fast as he could. When the situation didn't improve, Jane decided to homeschool him. An artist, she started a business making souvenir knickknacks, which gave her the flexibility to work from home. She painted Maine lighthouses on Christmas tree ornaments—and scrounged around for ways to meet her son's needs.

So began Jane's odyssey of guerrilla education. She didn't have a college degree. She and her husband gained and lost a series of jobs and never had much money. They prided themselves on being free spirits and often lived like pioneers in isolated rural areas, including for a while in a cabin without running water. They moved often to find employment. Despite these obstacles, Jane created a challenging education for her highly gifted son through some luck and a lot of perseverance. She joined a homeschooling group that she found by asking friends and neighbors. One day the homeschooling group was supposed to tour a local college campus. Somehow plans got mixed up, and Jane and Eric wound up at the college by themselves. They roamed the halls. A professor invited them into a classroom. When it became clear that Eric understood what was going on, another professor invited him to attend labs. So Eric started going to classes at the college, and Jane learned a lesson: Professors are often delighted to teach students who love to learn. "College professors are very intelligent people," she says. "They could understand. They'd say, 'Let's give him access to this information.' Administrative types would just say it's against the rules. I'd get nowhere with an official phone call."

Eventually, Eric realized he felt out of place in college classes and decided the idea was "weird." Through networking with friends, neighbors, teachers, and people from the college, Jane found a science tutor who charged an affordable fee for working with her son. This young man was studying to be a science teacher, and he told Jane he was getting as much out of the experience as Eric. One day he came to the cabin with the complete apparatus for distilling water. He and Eric assembled the contraption on the floor, merrily learning about the properties of water and scientific processes in a home with no plumbing of its own.

In Maine, the schools made old film strips available to homeschoolers, so Jane found some on the Apollo missions. They were hopelessly out of date, but Eric watched them, fascinated. One morning when Jane woke up, he told her he'd diagrammed the system for filtering carbon dioxide from the

Apollo capsule. He had made detailed drawings. She helped him find materials to set up a demonstration on the properties of carbon dioxide. He entered his project in a science fair and, at age seven, won first prize.

Soon they moved again, this time to Vermont. Without their previous social support network of homeschooling families, Jane and Eric spent a lot of quiet time together "unschooling." This unstructured learning worked well for both of them because it gave them time to daydream. "Eric," Jane says, "is totally self-motivated. Whatever outside direction you try to give him, it only goes so far. Sooner or later, whether that's in five minutes or six months, he comes up with his own thing." She wanted to go back to school to find a more settled career, so she looked for a school for Eric, but she didn't want to put him somewhere where he'd stare at the board and do whatever subjects were dictated on a daily basis from 9 A.M. to 3 P.M. She didn't want him in a school where he would only be given material he learned long ago. So they kept homeschooling while Jane started to homeschool herself—working toward a college degree through a distance-learning university.

Then, in the icy Vermont winter, she slipped and shattered her ankle. She and Eric went to stay with family in Maine while she recovered. There, while talking to her old friends, Jane found out about a summer program based on the Sudbury method of education—a progressive school model in which students learn what interests them at their own pace in an environment with rich resources. It sounded perfect for Eric, Jane said. Too bad it was only a summer program. But then a friend told her about a full-time school based on the Sudbury method with a bit more structure and incentives to ensure that children did learn. That school was based in Vermont.

Jane investigated, and soon Eric was enrolled, at age eleven, in this small, independent school of thirty students. Jane volunteered to help work off part of the tuition. Eric moved without much trouble from homeschooling to schooling and discovered a bonus: other gifted boys in the school close to his own age. They soon became close friends.

Through homeschooling, college classes, tutors, science experiments on the floor, and finally an appropriate school environment, Jane relied on her own flexibility. "The only constant thing in our lives is change," she says. But real learning can happen for gifted children with the help of parents and a caring intellectual community. "Look for other smart people," Jane says, "because they were once smart little people, too."

■ Can't Smart Kids Fend for Themselves?

Eric's family provides a model for parents who want to nurture their children's creativity and intelligence. Such nurturing doesn't take fancy degrees, but it does take energy and time—a lot of time. Few parents realize that nurturing their children's gifts—including advocating in their children's schools—is an ongoing, time-consuming process. It's also crucial. Research shows that parents play a more important role in the development of a child's gifts than schools. A supportive, advocating parent can make the difference between a meaningful education and wasted years.

Yet, like many educators and society at large, parents of gifted kids often think their children can fend for themselves. Some can. But many can't.

The most common problem that gifted kids face is under-achievement. With all the talk of failing schools these days, few consider that schools can shortchange their brightest, too. Most people think of underachievement as earning C's and D's on report cards or failing grade-level standardized tests. Some rebellious gifted children choose to show these behaviors, but even a child earning straight A's and scoring at the 99th percentile on grade-level tests is underachieving if she doesn't have to work for these accomplishments. These children may appear to be fending for themselves as they rack up honor roll mentions, become teachers' favorite pupils, and gain acceptance at good colleges. But when parents and teachers let children coast through school, they deny them one of life's greatest joys: setting a difficult goal, throwing oneself into the pursuit, and finally achieving it. These children never gain the self-confidence that comes from taking risks and stretching themselves. Many become perfectionists. They've never been challenged, so they've never failed and are petrified by the idea. According to the National Association for Gifted Children, as many as half of all gifted children meet this definition of underachievement.

Other children develop psychological problems in environments hostile to their gifts. Carlos didn't speak until he was three and a half years old, but when he did, he spoke in the complete sentences of a much older child. His mother, Debbi, who had been told her son might be autistic or retarded, couldn't believe a tester's diagnosis that he was actually gifted, so she brought home two-hundred-piece puzzles to see what he could do. Carlos put the puzzles together, starting from the center and working out. With incredible speed, he soon learned to read and write. His older brothers liked to tease him with math problems such as simple algebra or finding squares. Carlos teased back by figuring out the answers.

At school, however, the children spent hours learning to add single digits by grouping teddy bears. Carlos told his mother he didn't like kindergarten. He wanted to go to school to learn, but he hated the pointless work. By the end of the year he cried to stay home. The next year Debbi and the principal tried switching him between different classes to find a better match, but they had trouble finding a classroom that would tolerate this sensitive little boy who became upset when any child in the class was slighted. The other children teased him for being different and bookish, and wouldn't sit near him at lunch. Some bullies even beat him up. Carlos began to dread school. His hair started falling out, which his doctor said was from stress. He had trouble making friends. The other children were just learning to read while he read Roald Dahl's *Matilda* and dreamed of being a wizard at Hogwarts in the *Harry Potter* series. Meanwhile, the class droned through letters and numbers. He hated being different. He just wanted to be normal. This six-year-old boy started talking about how much better it would be if he were dumb . . . or dead.

Like Carlos, many gifted children become depressed when they lack intellectual peers and an appropriate educational environment. Although no studies have shown a higher rate of depression among moderately gifted children than non-gifted children, researchers have observed higher levels of depression and anxiety among children whose IQs place them four or more standard deviations above the norm (160+). Studies also indicate that there is a significantly higher incidence of mood disorders and suicide among gifted writers and visual artists. For many artistic individuals the line between psychosis and creativity is already blurry; always being an outsider in a school environment that doesn't value artistic gifts can push some students dangerously close to the edge.

Some gifted teenagers take up drinking or drug abuse in order to stay interested in life or numb the pain of being different; some engage in dangerous behaviors to gain the social acceptance that otherwise eludes them. Some become violent. The infamous school shooters had psychoses that begged to be treated, but many of them were also of above-average intelligence. Clay Shrout, who in 1994 murdered his family and took a class hostage at his school in Union, Kentucky, had a tested IQ of 160. At the sentencing hearing of Kip Kinkel, the Springfield, Oregon, school shooter, his psychiatrist noted, "He's cognitively bright, above average. Even though he has a learning disability, his overall IQ is high."

Certainly, not all neglected gifted children will lash out, but they will suffer. This suffering is particularly acute if the child has other special needs. Sharon, whose son Tim is dyslexic and profoundly gifted, insists that these children do not fend for themselves. When their talents are denied, "they end up frustrated and angry," she says. "That energy has to go somewhere else." Tim fell through the cracks in his school. Because he was so gifted, he could compensate for his inability to read. He earned normal grades. His teachers and counselors said he was so bright they never noticed his trouble reading. Because of his high achievement, the school wouldn't make such accommodations as books on tape. He could go to the special education class for a few hours a week, but school officials maintained that they were not required to accommodate his gifts. Sharon tried to appeal, but the school lawyer wouldn't show up. Meetings were canceled. "They didn't quibble with the idea that he was gifted and learning disabled," Sharon says. "It's just that it didn't matter. He needed to fail before he would be helped." Some even blamed his poor handwriting on laziness. After a while Tim simply lost his zeal. When his mom asked him to write a wish list for his seventh birthday, he broke into tears because writing was such a source of stress for him.

Eventually, she took him out of school—a difficult decision for a woman committed to public education. "I am the reluctant homeschooler," she says. "We were forced out of the public schools." She struggles with being a teacher and figuring out how to meet his needs. When she asked Tim to write "cream" on her chalkboard for a grocery list, he wrote "craem." She pointed out the misspelling. He just stared at her. As far as he could tell, he'd written exactly what she said. Yet he hung on every word of David McCullough's biography of John Adams when Sharon brought the tapes home. "Twice exceptional" children like Tim need schools that teach to their giftedness and accommodate their disabilities. But since their gifts and disabilities can cancel each other out and the child then functions roughly at grade level, many schools refuse to help. The tragedy of wasted time for these children is difficult to contemplate.

Gifted children from families with limited educational backgrounds may struggle in school if they don't know how high to set their goals. Some gifted minority students left to fend for themselves in environments that don't value learning are accused by peers of "acting white" for their achievements; they then have to choose between their giftedness and social acceptance. Gifted teenage girls may underachieve on purpose because they believe boys won't find them attractive if they win math contests. And any gifted child may struggle in a world that has little tolerance for those who are different.

Gifted kids can't fend for themselves because they are kids and have no legal rights of their own. But they shouldn't have to fend for themselves, because all children need to be nurtured to grow into happy, successful adults.

■ The Myth of the Pushy Parent

Parents form the first line of defense against the obstacles that gifted kids face in a society that often doesn't value their abilities. Gifted kids need a secure environment where they can be comfortable with their differences, and they need parents who support their zeal to learn and who can help them figure out which subjects and activities interest them most. Yet many parents simply trust that schools will educate children, thinking that a child's complaints about being bored or ostracized are just part of growing up. These parents worry that they'll be called "pushy" for advocating for their children.

Of course some parents demand unrealistic achievements or concern themselves too much with how the neighbors' children are faring. Some shuffle their kids around to too many lessons and practices. Gifted kids need daydreaming time to let thoughts percolate through their brains; these quiet moments are as important to growing as karate or Scouts.

But our experience is that more often gifted kids push their parents. The kids are the ones begging to try different extracurricular activities every day of the week. They're the ones asking questions, curious to probe deeper into how machines work or why people shiver when they're cold. They're the ones standing on tiptoe to reach the adult-level books from the top shelf. While parents of moderately gifted children may regale coworkers and friends with tales of their children's precocity, the brighter the child the more likely the parent is to just keep quiet.

Bragging about one's child is a birthright of being a parent—when she took her first step, said her first word, learned how to read. But friendly bragging in the neighborhood and at work involves a quid pro quo. You talk about your kid for a bit, then I'll talk about mine. If you can't talk about the same thing, the bragging stops. Parents who are proud of an A on a test resent hearing about another kid who has just skipped three grades, published an academic paper, and still complains that the work is too easy. Schools don't want to hear it, either. "Most parents of gifted children who have legitimate and valid reasons for demanding curriculum alteration for their children *do not* ever approach the school for fear of being labeled pushy or because they feel that since their child has exceptional ability, they should simply be grateful," says Nicholas Colangelo, a professor of gifted education at the University of Iowa.

Mary, mother of Zach, tells us, "I always downplayed it when I realized how unique he was. It seemed boastful. Acknowledging it is almost like coming out of the closet." Zach, when evacuated from their isolated Alaskan homestead during an asthma attack at age nine months, saw his stats flashing on the medical monitors. When they read "6-6" he said, "Same." When they changed, he said, "Different." When he was a toddler, Mary took him to the local docks to see the boats putter out to sea. He'd become quite agitated that the letters and numbers on the boats' sides were out of order. How could she explain that agitation to other mothers bringing their children to see the boats glide over the water? Now that Zach is older, she still doesn't like talking about his gifts. "There's an undercurrent: You're so smart, shouldn't you be perfect at everything? Because in our society it's okay to be smart, but you don't want to be that different," she says.

No parent, however pushy, can force a nine-month-old baby to articulate whether numbers are the same or different. Often, parents just want their kids to be normal. One mother we know who tried to help her highly gifted son with math said that she felt like a "tractor next to a freight train." She wrote notes in her journal, such as "The psychologist says that for John's high IQ (the number I did not want to know), he thinks he is very well adjusted." When the local gifted program offered to accept her seven-year-old into fourth grade, she balked. "I don't see that as an option." A school administrator told the family that "she has worked with a few kids like John before, but he is the only happy child among them. She said we must be doing a good job. What a nice thing for her to say—and how I need that!"

Another mother, Catherine, says her son Sam made her realize that she simply couldn't be a pushy parent. She saw another parent jogging with his son, shouting multiplication tables back and forth to make sure the boy learned them. "Sam just learned them," Catherine says. "I didn't do a thing."

When kids push the parents, parents worry whether anyone will truly accept their children, even outside of school. Lucy, who grew up on a North Dakota air force base, learned to read the *Little House on the Prairie* books on her own shortly after her fourth birthday. Her mom, Samantha, saw a list of kindergarten exit goals that a neighbor's child brought home. Lucy had already achieved those goals at age three. Not knowing how gifted her child was, Samantha marveled that other parents thought these goals were normal—but she soon learned that she couldn't share this thought with the neighbors. Lucy skipped two grades and did well in second grade, but the next year her third grade teacher was so uncomfortable with the idea of a younger child in her class that she said the placement would "destroy" the girl and that she would be better off out of the classroom.

So Samantha started homeschooling. But in the close-knit community of a military base, a profoundly gifted child, even one not enrolled in the local school, still makes people uneasy. "I avoid talking about academics or anything achievement-related at all," Samantha tells us. "Sports seem safe, but even there I feel like it is seen as inappropriate for me to say too much 'good' about her. I worry about this because I want her to hear me say good things about her, but it is so uncomfortable. I completely avoid talking about grade placement and age in the same conversation. I've noticed Lucy shies away from answering people when they ask what grade she's in. I'm sure she feels the tension when she answers and they start computing what that means." That tension makes everything more difficult, from questions at neighborhood functions to finding friends who don't see the child as strange.

But highly gifted kids can never be "normal." We run an on-line bulletin board where the children we work with can discuss various topics. Recently, puzzle designer Scott Kim worked with some of the kids to invent puzzles for *Discover* magazine. Eleven-year-olds suggested modular math riddles. A six-year-old tried forming sequences with the number of letters in each element in the periodic table. These children use bigger words than their age peers. They move more rapidly through stages of mental development and learn to reason and understand abstract concepts long before other children. They absorb the world in an entirely different way.

■ Becoming a Child's Advocate

As Jane, Eric's mom, discovered, finding an appropriate education for a highly gifted child doesn't have to be expensive (though it can be). As one parent says, "These children can be trusted to learn above and beyond practically by themselves with a library card." Dreamy hours huddled between the stacks in the local library can be among the most pleasant moments of childhood. Medieval castles and distant galaxies stretch the mind more than most classrooms.

Parents can make sure their children have access to all the educational resources their communities offer. This can mean sitting in the back during lectures at a local college, or finding professionals in town who work in whatever fields interest the child. Most people are flattered to be asked to discuss their work with a curious student. Cities contain all sorts of wonders, from museums to concerts, but even in rural areas the Internet has made finding interesting material easier than ever for parents of gifted kids. Classic texts with expired copyrights have been made available online, or one can just type "Egyptology" into Google and land among the pyramids faster than any flight to Cairo.

Parents can make sure they know what their children are learning in school and can decide whether this matches their children's ability levels. If not, parents need to learn to advocate for their children. When a parent suspects a child is gifted, the first step is to have the child assessed by an educational psychologist to determine his or her needs. Many school districts have on staff a coordinator for gifted and talented students who can advise you on testing and assessment options. (Please see www.GeniusDenied.com for information on testing and assessment.) Research shows that parents are usually correct in guessing their child's precocity. If anything, they underestimate. According to Gina Ginsberg and Charles Harrison's *How to Help Your Gifted Child*, "There are more parents who have gifted children and don't know it than there are parents who don't have gifted children but think they do."

Families we know who have negotiated successful situations in their schools recommend reading the research on effective practices and bringing in highlighted copies of relevant articles for teachers and administrators. They recommend knowing the school district and its policies, philosophies, and buzzwords. They recommend creating a list of what needs to change for the child to receive a challenging, appropriate education, but also leaving room for negotiation and alternative ideas that teachers and administrators propose. Such changes include going to a different grade-level class for a subject or two, going to the library to read instead of doing reading worksheets, using a distance-learning curriculum such as Stanford's Education Program for Gifted Youth for some subjects, or having the teacher create more in-depth assignments such as long-term research or creative writing projects. (For more ideas, please see www.GeniusDenied.com.)

Many parents ask for their child to skip a grade or two, presenting this option as a way for the school to meet the child's educational needs without changing the curriculum or providing in-class enrichment. Successful advocates remain pleasant and accommodating and always thank school officials for their professionalism. They also promise to support the school, either by volunteering in the child's classroom or another one that needs help or by assisting with after-school programs or in some other way. They help the school meet their child's needs by spending their own time finding appropriate books and curricular materials, and purchasing these materials if the parent's financial circumstances allow that.

Successful parents also learn to think outside of the educational box. Sometimes this means homeschooling. About half of the families we work with choose this option at some point during their child's kindergarten-to-twelfth-grade schooling experience. They don't just learn at home. Most have some experience with their local schools and combine at-home learning with other resources in the community, including school programs, college classes, tutors, and distance learning. For instance, a child may attend elementary school in the afternoon for gym class, art, and music with other children of the same age, and then cover the academic subjects at home. Or a child may attend calculus class at the local high school and literature at the local middle school, and then study Spanish with a neighbor who speaks the language fluently. Families move in and out of home-, public, and private schooling as each matches the child's ability levels. Flexibility is key. As May, mother of Jill, says, "Homeschooling an extremely gifted child is daunting. What works today is guaranteed not to work in six months. 'Canned' curricula are useless. Every single day is a challenging adventure."

Jill's family lives in a small, financially strapped district. The aluminum mill, which provided most of the tax base, closed in recent years, and so the local schools have suffered through various cuts and restructuring. Yet to May's amazement this uncertainty has actually given caring educators the freedom to take risks to help Jill's hybrid homeschooling and schooling education work.

Jill's precocity stood out from the beginning, although since she was a firstborn, May blamed her amazement on the blindness of mother love. When Jill was one, she made jokes like "Look, Mama, I have toe food!" when she dipped her foot in mashed tofu on her high chair tray. If she coughed a few times, she'd say, "I guess I drank too much coffee."

At age two she became an expert on volcanology, drawing pictures of the tectonic plates and the Pacific Rim. She would play with her Duplo building blocks and say, "Guess what, Mommy. Three fours make twelve!" while looking at the knobs. She composed songs on her Little Tikes piano, then wrote down the notes using the colors of the keys and different-shaped marks to represent the notes. She was not interested in preschool, but May thought she should go. She mostly hated it, and the teacher did not like her; Jill corrected her scientific facts with the limited tact of a four-year-old.

After preschool, Jill went to a private elementary school for kindergarten through the third grade. She gradually lost her spark. Teachers made her do simple rote work. Her third grade teacher said she was "just terrible at math." Yet around this time May found Jill tuned in to NPR one night when she was supposed to be asleep. She was listening to Philip Glass lecture on how he used mathematical concepts to compose. She begged to stay up because she found it so interesting and meaningful. Meanwhile, Jill was having nightmares in which she'd open a closet and find herself dismembered. May guessed that this recurrent dream was all about changing herself—cutting herself up—to fit into the mold of a third grade girl.

So May took Jill out of private school, homeschooled her for four days a week, and on the fifth day had her attend the public school's pull-out gifted program for enrichment, which the local school psychologist approved. The teacher there understood Jill better than anyone else; she also enjoyed having her around and found interesting projects for her to pursue. At first the rest of the week centered on ending the nightmares and putting Jill back together again. Lesson plans included how to make a tuna fish sandwich and painting the solar system to scale on a long roll of paper. Gradually they built back up to an academic curriculum, with May adjusting the lesson plans she found to fit Jill's passions. They eventually moved to a new district and found the local school's pull-out program open to Jill's part-time attendance as well. This teacher, too, wanted Jill to have the best education possible.

When Jill was eleven, May asked about enrolling her in French at the local high school. Her pull-out teacher, the elementary school psychologist, and another administrator encouraged her to try. The high school assistant principal was speechless when May phoned to ask, but the other educators assured him that Jill was capable of the work and that she should be welcome in any class she chose. He met the family. When he asked Jill about her career plans, she replied that she wanted to be a high-energy astrophysicist, an Egyptologist, or an animal behavior specialist. Her animation and maturity convinced the man to give this crazy plan a whirl.

Jill took French, biology, and orchestra at the high school while taking a distance-learning course in algebra. At first students kept asking Jill her age, but eventually most students decided it was cool to have "some kind of genius" in the class. She did get teased but learned to dismiss the taunts as others' insecurity. In time she started receiving phone calls from classmates asking for help on their French and biology homework. Students sought her as a lab partner.

Jill's first semester worked so well that she asked to attend high school full-time—the equivalent of a three- to four-year acceleration. And the experience worked well enough for the school district to start seeing itself as the kind of flexible place that encouraged different approaches. May had to "jump through hoops and wade through meeting after meeting for a couple of years," but most likely the family of the next highly gifted child will not. Advocacy will bear fruit long after the first child moves on.

May recommends being as helpful and polite as possible while ladling out praise when things go well. Most of the families we've worked with have found that they get nowhere if they approach a school claiming an appropriate education is their child's right since in most states such an education *isn't* a right. Some school districts will refuse to help regardless of the parent's attitude; Jane and Sharon got nowhere with some of the schools they tried despite presenting research, plans, and pleasant faces. But other schools respond to gratitude. May realizes that Jill's fortune stems from a couple of caring educators who didn't mind going the extra miles for them repeatedly. Still, "Every single time I have a positive encounter with anyone in this school district, I make sure to compliment everyone on their flexibility and creative thinking," May says. "Next time they are even more accommodating."

■ Finding Intellectual Peers

Perhaps the most important thing parents can do to meet their gifted kids' needs is provide them with opportunities to be with their intellectual peers so they can develop true friendships. Some parents assume highly gifted children should just become fast friends with other children in their school classes or neighborhood. Some chide their gifted children for being antisocial when they choose solitude. But many of these children have little in common with their classmates other than age. An eighth grade girl who wants to share her ideas about politics and novels will have little to talk about with classmates who prefer to discuss the new store at the mall.

Gifted kids are acutely aware that they are different. The most confident ones shrug it off, but more wonder "What's wrong with me?" This question rarely leads to a positive self-concept. The more precocious the child, the worse the disconnect becomes. The most highly gifted face what gifted education expert Miraca Gross calls a "forced-choice dilemma": achievement or friendship. Gifted children often hide their intelligence to blend in. Those who choose achievement must learn to live with having only a few good friends, who tend to be several years older. Even then, life circumstances can make friendship more difficult. Jill struggled to make friends at the high school even though she fit in better there than she did with her age peers. Many radically accelerated gifted children discover that being years younger than classmates makes them less strange than being years older intellectually. But neither is easy.

When we started working with gifted children, our chief mission was to help families nurture their children's talents, but we soon discovered that these families most appreciated meeting a community of other people facing similar challenges and joys. Now we bring our young scholars and their parents together for annual gatherings. At these weekend retreats, kids forge friendships with true peers, and parents find others who can empathize with their experiences. Eight-year-olds talk about physics while building sand castles. They don't have to translate their thoughts into smaller words. They don't have to hide their intelligence to fit in. Humans naturally crave the friendship of others like them; gifted children likewise need friends who don't leave them asking themselves, "What's wrong with me?" At our Lake Tahoe gathering a few years ago, a starry-eyed Jill told her parents, "I've finally found my co-planeteers."

When they can't be together in person, these families stay in touch through the online community we've created, where parents can share support and information. Some of these families even form regional organizations so they can continue to meet and learn from one another. The Hobbits and Wizards, for instance, descended on a farm in central Massachusetts on a November weekend in 2002 to play and share their stories. As soon as the cars pulled off the winding country road and parked by the farmhouse, a Capture the Flag game with old corncobs commenced in the backyard. The children, ages nine to eleven, dashed shrieking between the barns and raced toward a nearby beaver pond. One of the ten-year-old children crashing through a leaf pile had already attended college for math. Another had written a novel. One child with severe learning disabilities was so precocious that he managed to mask his learning disabilities so teachers never noticed them. These children and others reveled in hayrides and card games and the strange comfort of being around others who saw them as "normal."

Their parents talked over coffee in the kitchen. They shared their combat scars from battling bureaucracies and told happier stories of partnering with understanding teachers and schools. One mother confessed that she had never thought she'd be homeschooling: that was for families with religious or political objections to public schools. People recounted the stares they received when neighbors found out their preteens were already considering college. One father said his local school assigned an aide to a child with behavioral problems so that child could have a positive educational experience. Meanwhile, the school refused to provide accelerated classes for that father's son and let him rot in a classroom that failed to challenge him. That family started homeschooling, too. Families recounted school administrators' assurances that they had several children as bright as theirs who were doing just fine with grade-level work, so why were these parents complaining? Or that the school had "one child" years ago who was accelerated in some subjects, but it turned out to be a disaster. So they won't do it again despite the ongoing disaster of the status quo.

Families of highly gifted children hear these excuses constantly from schools, districts, and society. In the outside world, children such as Carlos, Jill, the Hobbits and Wizards, and others learn to hide their abilities and, faced with America's race toward the lowest common denominator, wish they could be normal. So parents have to guide their children into developing their gifts. They have to coax and cajole schools into providing an appropriate education for their children. They have to help children find friends and let them play and talk and grow in places where no one sees them as freaks. At the Hobbits and Wizards gathering in Massachusetts, these kids could finally be kids. One mother couldn't stop crying as she saw her son playing happily, his burdens scattered like the November leaves.

Chapter 5

Patrons, Teachers, and Mentors

B ARRY JEKOWSKY, maestro of the California Symphony, began his musical career as a four-year-old in Brooklyn who tried desperately to play his father's trumpet. His little lungs couldn't make a sound from the instrument, but that didn't stop the young maestro from puffing up his cheeks and blowing. He wanted to learn. He wanted to make those same glorious sounds as his amateur musician father and brother. He was exuberant about music. He couldn't *not* play.

At age five he began to study the piano and percussion. Music came easily to the little brown-haired boy, and by the time he was eight, two of his teachers had thrown up their hands and told his parents that they had no more to teach him. A neighboring family had sent their son to Juilliard, so Jekowsky's parents took him there. He auditioned and won a full scholarship to the school's precollege program. For the first year his parents drove him every Saturday to Juilliard's old home near Columbia University on Manhattan's Upper West Side. By the time he was ten he had learned to ride the subway train by himself from Brooklyn. He made that journey for a decade, through his elementary and high school years.

Juilliard welcomed Jekowsky into a long, romantic history of musical instruction—one musician guiding another's hands over strings or keys, and then the younger musician in turn guiding another's. "The mentoring process is a natural tradition in music," Jekowsky says. Talented adults recognize talented children and understand the need to nurture them in both the techniques and beauty of their art. The system isn't perfect, especially in finding children who don't grow up around music or who live far from master teachers. Still, teachers and mentors help grow new artists in every generation who develop their talent at far younger ages than is possible in most other fields. The education system in America has a lot to learn from the musical tradition if we want to nurture genius in whatever subject it occurs.

Jekowsky savored his luck to be musically gifted and living in New York City as he soaked up all Juilliard offered, shuttling between instruments, learning conducting, poring over theory books, and studying how the sounds work together. Soon he was taking classes three times a week after school. He started landing professional engagements. When he was fourteen, a mentor convinced the *Man of La Mancha* orchestra to let him play with them in the pit for that Broadway show. Jekowsky was living the life of a musician.

From the beginning, teachers at Juilliard spotted his interest in the overall orchestral scheme; he once even rescored his high school alma mater. They nurtured his conducting talent. One teacher bought him tickets to performances of visiting orchestras just so he could see conductors that the teacher thought were important. Legendary Juilliard violin instructor Dorothy DeLay met Jekowsky and saw a spark of his ability. When she organized concerto concerts for her students at the Aspen Music Festival, which he started attending at age sixteen, she asked him to conduct. He did. "The people in those concertos are now the who's who of violin playing today," he says.

He joined the Juilliard college program. An instructor he knew from the precollege program, James Wimer, asked him to keep Thursdays free to study solfègse (the noninstrumental part of music: ear training, theory, analysis, rhythmic development, and the like) with him. They would sometimes work from nine in the morning until ten at night as the young maestro learned the secrets of composers and conductors past. "He saw in me something so special that he was willing to invest an entire day in me" every week for three years, Jekowsky says of his teacher. He wouldn't forget that gift.

After completing the master's program at Juilliard, Jekowsky became the principal tympanist for the San Francisco Symphony and the youngest member of that orchestra at the time. He founded the California Symphony soon after. He became the associate conductor of the National Symphony Orchestra in Washington, D.C. He became the music director of the Reno Philharmonic. He started guest-conducting orchestras worldwide. He began winning awards and critical praise. And once he achieved these positions of influence, he made sure to return his old instructors' favors.

When we talked with Jekowsky recently, he had just made calls to persuade the director of a summer program to squeeze a talented young viola player onto the roster after she missed the application deadline. The director asked for a videotape to be express-mailed to her; after listening to the young woman's amazing command of her instrument, she found her a spot.

Jekowsky began finding prodigies and arranging their professional debuts long before that became the fashionable thing for orchestras to do. He wanted young musicians to experience real quality rather than the mediocre student orchestras that often accompany their solos. Young Sarah Chang, at age nine, joined the California Symphony in her pink party dress to play Tchaikovsky's violin concerto on her pint-sized violin. Sarah beamed with the fun of it all. "It's exciting for the young people, but how exciting for those who can see their first performances?" Jekowsky asks. Sarah soon became a star, a regular A-list performer with orchestras around the world. Jekowsky arranged similar concerts for violinists Kyoko Takezawa and Leila Josefowicz, pianist Helen Huang, and cellist Alisa Weilerstein. He continues to do so for many others.

He also started the Young American Composer in Residence program at the California Symphony in 1991, a unique mentoring partnership that Jekowsky considers his proudest musical achievement. "We complain about American music, but we haven't done anything to help composers," he says. His young composers experiment in the "orchestra-laboratory" that Jekowsky has created, working closely with professional musicians to grow their works from idea to world premiere performance. The entire orchestra mentors these artists. Composers including Kamran Ince, Chris Theofanidis, Kevin Puts, and Pierre Jalbert have graduated from the program to win the prestigious Rome Prize. Jalbert recently won the Master Prize from the BBC in London.

Gifts, Jekowsky says, are "part of the beauty of life." He enjoys watching his prodigies bloom just as a gardener savors his flowers. He loves to see their drive to succeed. "Musicians are workaholics. They love to learn, love to improve. 'I know this today,' we say. 'What can I learn tomorrow?'" Even Leonard Bernstein, whom Jekowsky encountered in his later days, was always trying to figure out how to "get it." That desire to improve leads to wanting others to improve as well. Jekowsky won't call it an obligation. "When you are successful as a musician, you feel wealthy, not in a monetary sense, in an enlightened sense. You feel full of life, happy, as though you've received a gift." And so people want to share that gift. "I know if I didn't have people who listened, people who saw my needs, I wouldn't have this wonderful life I have. It's something you do because you believe in it, because others believed in you," he says.

■ Making Music in Other Fields

The music model of recognizing talent and finding master teachers who can give young people access to knowledge and expect the most from them can be replicated in other fields. As we've said before, American schools are responsible for an appalling waste of time and talent among bright students. Yet within this maze of dumbed-down classes and indifferent schools lurks a more insidious obstacle for highly gifted kids: America's insistence on a broad, general curriculum every year from kindergarten through grade twelve. As a free society we hate the thought of cutting off options early in life, and we romanticize the idea of a jack-of-all-trades. American schools pledge to educate everyone and expose students to a wide variety of topics. It's easier to make a broad curriculum shallow rather than deep, so few schools allow students to specialize much before college.

But the goal of education—to form a productive, democratic citizen—does not take all thirteen years for highly gifted children. These children do not need to plod through English 7, followed by English 8 and English 9, as night follows day, with no one asking why. This plodding doesn't force children to keep their options open. Instead, it squelches them. A gifted young writer needs more than just an assignment every few weeks to write a haiku and illustrate it. His teacher doesn't nurture his talent by writing "Super!" in red pen simply because his five-paragraph essay is better than the other children's musings. She doesn't nurture his talent by reminding him to be creative. He will learn to be creative on his own as he writes short stories at night solely for the love of it, cranks out a draft of a novel in his spare time, and scribbles poems in the margins of his math notes.

A gifted, creative child needs that creativity honed and trained. He needs to learn grammar. He needs to have his work critiqued by other talented writers. He needs to learn how to edit himself and organize his thoughts, to learn how word choice can help a composition soar. He doesn't need to stop writing when the bell rings after the allotted forty-five minutes so that he can go to the next class and spend an equal amount of time learning geography or health.

Likewise, a young mathematician needs to learn the subject's tricks, the ways of constructing proofs, and the beauty of neat solutions. Scientists need to learn lab techniques and how to find problems that aren't posed as end-of-chapter questions. Research shows that childhood and the teen years are crucial for talent development. If children don't learn the skills of their crafts when they are young enough to let such knowledge become second nature, they will not forge as far ahead as they could later in life. Basic education for highly talented students needs to be condensed to allow time for their passions to be identified and pursued. This already happens with gymnasts and actors. Precocious mathematical talent is just as important.

World-class performance in any field demands intense efforts—four hours of practice a day, for instance—for a decade or more. That may sound like a lot, and it may conjure images of parents hovering as a child cranks out equations for the proper number of hours, but the average child in America watches four hours of television a day. Society needs world-class scientists more than it needs world-class couch potatoes.

Musicians have an easier time fitting this model of specialization and learning with master teachers, Jekowsky says, because most people don't study music in school. Students come to the art on their own, and so parents and other adults accept the idea of individual instruction and acceleration based on the child's talents. Since they've already found one teacher for lessons, they'll find another to help the child learn more when she exhausts the expertise of the first. With school subjects, parents and teachers are more likely to see a bright student and think, "Isn't it nice that she's earning A's?" and let her continue with the standard five hours per subject per week. Meanwhile, the child's feverish mind must try to nurture her own talent, scribbling poetry in her notebooks, working equations everywhere, or poring over a biology text hidden under a desk, since according to the almighty schedule, she can study only history from 10:15 to 11:05 every morning.

This is a waste, and talent wasted is talent denied. Parents must recognize and nurture their children's gifts; they form the first line of defense against such squandering. But others in society also have an obligation to nurture gifted children. On an individual level, children suffer when their talents are neglected. They fail to become the successful, happy adults they could be. But society suffers, too, by letting crops rot during a famine. Society needs its dreamers to write novels and symphonies, to develop new drugs and inventions. Patrons, teachers, and mentors need to be available to assist and guide gifted kids. They need to help them identify and nurture their talents.

Jekowsky likes to use the analogy of parents as the general contractor for their children's talents. The contractor is most important to the building process, but the contractor has to find others—electricians, carpenters, plumbers, masons—to construct the reaching skyscraper of a gifted child's life.

■ Finding Talent

For talent to be nurtured by teachers and mentors, it has to be found. How does anyone—including the child—know if her talents make her the top mathematician in her school or in the city, the state, or the nation? Since most schools don't have a differentiated enough or advanced enough curriculum to know a child's true ability, competitions and talent searches can fill the void if people pay attention to the results. Plus, contests are a powerful motivating force to develop talent—everyone likes to win. Because teachers and others often coach students for contests, these contests provide an opportunity for mentoring.

The best competitions reach large numbers of students and have several levels of difficulty to provide feedback for parents and teachers. Among the most famous are the talent searches run by universities for middle school students. Since 1972, when Professor Julian Stanley of Johns Hopkins University first gave high-achieving middle schoolers college entrance exams to find exceptional potential, more than 1 million children have participated in talent searches run by universities such as Northwestern, the University of Iowa, the University of Denver, and Duke. These students usually take the SAT or the ACT, which are aimed at high school juniors and seniors. Although all search participants must score above the 95th percentile on their grade-level tests, some will score only the minimum on the SAT and ACT, and others will have near perfect results. These scores can then determine which students need more advanced work than they are receiving.

At least that's the idea. Almost nowhere does this happen in practice. A more typical result is that of a young man named Stephen. He did well enough on the SAT as a seventh grader to cover algebra and geometry during a talent search program he took the following summer. Then he started eighth grade and went right back into algebra class. "Some people may have argued more," he says, "but the school made you jump through hoops, and there was no class past algebra in the middle school."

Talent search programs have fought this attitude for years. "Julian Stanley saw this from the beginning," says Susan Assouline of the Belin-Blank Center for Gifted Education and Talent Development at the University of Iowa. "There have been very slight changes. Now it's no longer phenomenally radical to take algebra in eighth grade." That, of course, won't satisfy a kid who is capable of more.

But even if schools don't use the information they receive from talent search scores, these searches at least let the middle school student and her parents know more about her abilities. The talent search programs themselves award high scorers with scholarships, and their summer programs can nurture the brightest, even if that's only for three weeks a year. At these summer camps students can meet master teachers who specialize in stoking the flames of gifted children's curiosity. Many keep in touch with their students during the school year.

The national Math Counts competition also finds talent among middle schoolers. Schools field teams for local competitions. The winners of these competitions compete at the state level and then form state teams to compete at the national level.

We know parents who have formed and coached teams when teachers and administrators didn't have an interest in the competition, in order to give young "mathletes" the opportunity to learn more math than they would in school and to pit their skills against the brightest students nationwide.

Other competitions find and nurture talent at more advanced levels. The American Math, Physics, and Chemistry Olympiad programs find exceptionally talented youngsters by administering progressively more grueling exams in these subjects to high school students. The highest two dozen or so scorers convene in a central location over the summer for training and coaching. The top handful of these young people compete against students from other countries in the International Olympiads for gold, silver, and bronze medals, just as sports stars do in the conventional Olympics. (See www.GeniusDenied.com for details on competitions.)

Students get much more out of these contests than their medals and trophies. The contests help students realize just how talented they are. A study of these math and science Olympians, for instance, found that 76 percent said they would not have accomplished as much without the Olympiad programs. The same percentage, and 83 percent of their parents, thought the program increased their awareness of educational opportunities. As the study found, "Some of [the Olympians] had undervalued their capabilities and had set more modest goals for themselves. Their high scores on the Olympiad exams supplied them with much more confidence in their abilities." The scores let them know their own potential and that they could consider themselves among the most promising mathematicians and scientists in the country, or perhaps the world. Olympians also reported that they enjoyed being exposed to other equally bright peers during the training phases and loved hearing presentations by well-known scientists and mathematicians. These relationships with successful adults helped them understand what they could do with their talents.

Contests such as the Intel Talent Search and competitions for scholarships such as the Davidson Fellows award encourage students to do research over the summer by offering large and prestigious prizes for original results. Musically talented students have many contests open to them, and special schools are also available if they live in major metropolitan areas. Statewide contests can identify talent, as can all-state orchestras and bands.

Unfortunately, many other competitions don't receive widespread publicity and therefore don't attract enough entries to find truly top talent. Local newspapers chart the successes of a hometown basketball team that is progressing toward the state championship, but few academic contests can say the same of their winners—and so others don't know about these kids or think to enter the competitions. And too many contests, such as some essay competitions sponsored by corporations, civic organizations, and government departments, choose their winners based on adherence to a pre-chosen theme, not creativity and quality.

When done right, competitions and talent searches can find students with exceptional potential, but even the most talented individual, if not coached, will do less well in a contest than she could. And if a contest identifies talent but the child's talent isn't nurtured, that is just as big a waste as if the talent were never found at all. When this happens, you have kids simply living for these contests and for the short programs during the summer that talent searches and Olympiads offer. Liz Baker, who helped teach a drama and writing class in a talent search program at Stanford, says her students "were like camels who find a lake in the desert—drinking up all the water they could in the short time they had."

■ **Mentoring Genius**

Dedicated teachers can keep students from needing to turn into the "camels" that Baker saw. Mentors have been around since the original Mentor tutored lonely and inquisitive Telemachus while his father, Odysseus, was off fighting at Troy. Athena, goddess of wisdom, would transform herself into the boy's mentor and guide his decisions as he grew. Since those mythical days, caring individuals have shaped the lives of many talented youngsters throughout history.

Frederic Chopin's teacher famously devoted his life to the young composer. Annie Sullivan tapped Helen Keller's gifts in her dark and silent world. Albert Camus, author of *The Stranger* and *The Plague*, grew up frightfully poor in Algeria. His tutor, Louis Germain, recognized his giftedness and brought him books. He persuaded Camus's family to let him attend high school. When Camus years later won the Nobel Prize for literature, he wrote to Germain, "Without you, without the affectionate hand you extended to the small, poor child that I was, without your teaching and your example, none of all this would have happened."

Some individuals make a career of doing what Germain did—finding exceptional talent and helping gifted young people become noticed on the world stage. The legendary violin teacher Dorothy DeLay at Juilliard coached generations of musicians, among them Barry Jekowsky and Sarah Chang, before she died in 2002. An exceptionally gifted person herself, DeLay discovered her calling as a teacher. In addition to helping students learn all the techniques of musicality, she helped them develop their own voices so they learned to make the music sing. She developed many teaching principles over time: teaching by encouragement, exposing the child to many different styles instead of imposing the teacher's, encouraging open communication and feedback, introducing the pleasure of the art, teaching determination, and helping children set lofty goals.

You don't have to go to Juilliard to find teachers willing to nurture and develop the talents of highly gifted young people. They exist in schools everywhere. Wenyi, a highly accomplished young woman, went to a traditional high school in Illinois. The school offered numerous AP classes and humanities electives, but Wenyi still felt she had outgrown the school by her junior year. The curriculum didn't challenge her. The school didn't value intellectual talents as it could have. Once, an assembly intended to honor many student accomplishments became a rally for the football team, which had narrowly missed winning the state championship. Wenyi had just won a national science award, but the principal forgot to bring her plaque.

In her sophomore year Wenyi met her journalism teacher, who was to become a major influence in her life. They didn't like each other at first and fought a number of skirmishes over assignments, but soon they came to recognize each other's talents. Her teacher, Wenyi says, was never content just to run a high school newspaper. She wanted to win awards—national awards. "There are a lot of things in life that if you don't think about, they'll never come to you," Wenyi says. "She taught me to dream big." She helped Wenyi hone her writing. She encouraged her to attempt big stories on subjects such as teens losing parents, plagiarism, and dating violence. She pushed Wenyi to enter contests and, sure enough, she won them. As Wenyi pushed herself to try more and more new contests, activities, and research projects through high school, her journalism teacher kept her levelheaded and sane. Wenyi always preferred friends who were several years older, and as these students graduated, she became disconnected from her high school's social scene. However, she and her teacher would talk for hours after school about life, the universe, everything.

Wenyi also found a mentor to teach her science and math skills that went far beyond her high school's offerings. She wanted to try an original scientific research project, so she and her parents made inquiries. Dr. Jin Wang, a friend of a friend, was enlisted to see if Wenyi could work with him at the Argonne National Laboratory in Argonne, Illinois. She couldn't be a full-time intern because she wasn't in college, so Dr. Wang had to work hard to give her a chance in his lab. He, too, was skeptical of what she'd be able to do. He'd never worked with a high schooler before, so the first week she was at Argonne, he assigned her a mathematical modeling problem he thought would take her all summer. She figured it out in a week. He then assigned another problem. She did this one in a week too. This step-by-step introduction helped her grasp the scientific process of figuring out problems without checkable solutions in the back of the textbook. "There was no guarantee I was going to be able to get it," she says.

But she did, and soon she was ready to work on a full-fledged project. She used those same mathematical skills to model gasoline sprays for fuel-injection technology, using computer programming to transform thousands of lines of code into three-dimensional images. She would program for hours on her computer at home, starting at 10 A.M. and working late into the night. She would simply lose herself in the lines of letters and numbers. Sometimes their secrets eluded her, and hours turned into failure and frustration—and determination, as she refused to go to sleep before she found what she wanted. But other times the lines suddenly would make sense, taking form, answering her questions. She worked hard, but she loved it. Dr. Wang was the busiest person in the lab and never let an opportunity pass him by, Wenyi says. She wanted to do the same.

By the end of the summer they figured out that the gasoline spray was not uniform but contained many intense concentrations. She kept working on the research after she went to school that fall, sometimes sleeping only three hours a night. But it made her happy. And others began to notice, too. Her research has now found Department of Energy funding and interest from automobile companies in Detroit. With Dr. Wang's encouragement, she started collecting scientific awards to complement her journalism ones. "He first gave me an opportunity and that had a snowballing effect—it profoundly affected my life," Wenyi says. "Obviously, I had to seize it and make something of it." But without a research mentor who checked his skepticism about a high school student, she would not have had the experience she did. He maintained his support for her all through the project, and his high expectations made her dream big, too. "I felt that if I didn't exceed his expectations, I'd disappoint him," she says.

Wenyi has very supportive parents, but these mentors changed her high school career by helping her find opportunities for winning national recognition. Otherwise, she'd think she was just a pretty bright student who had managed to come in second in her high school class.

▉ Learning Partners

More than anything else, highly gifted children need understanding, says Ron Young, executive director of the Western
Pennsylvania Cyber Charter School, where a seven-year-old boy
we know named Vijay is enrolled. The Cyber Charter School was
designed for all sorts of special needs children and homeschoolers, but Young, a former high school administrator, made sure it
would work for highly gifted children too. As soon as he met
Vijay, he brainstormed how he and Vijay's parents could nurture
his talents together. "I was so happy to have had the program in
which he could grow," Young says. He chucked the standard curriculum and found a new one for Vijay. He suggested books and
topics for research projects. He found the resources to make
these projects work, and he started inviting Vijay to give presentations to the Cyber Charter School staff. "He has to communicate his work to others," Young says. Vijay simply can't keep his
thoughts bottled up. These presentations to adult audiences have
also helped the boy gain confidence. Recently, Vijay played his violin at a conference for charter school administrators. The audience of hundreds never fazed him. He even informed the
president of the organization—who had made a too hasty move
toward the podium—that he had another selection to perform.

Too often, Young says, highly gifted students are put in situations where they are unable to grow. "I prayed that we wouldn't
make any mistakes with this young man," he says. "Enrichment
activities are not enough for these children. Teachers sometimes fall back on the rote memory type of things for their
classes, but they quickly learn that they lose the gifted kids."
Those like Young who make an effort to teach differently and
who find time to work one-on-one with gifted students can
change these children's lives.

The gifted students we've worked with often tell us of people like Young who go out of their way to help them simply because they can't stand to see talent squandered. After four semesters of taking college science courses on nights and weekends for enrichment, Jacob, age twelve, had taken all he could at the introductory level. He needed more advanced math to take the university's higher level science courses, so his parents called the math department and made an appointment with the assistant chairman. The assistant chairman reviewed Jacob's test scores with a math education specialist and decided that Jacob was bright enough to complete all his high school math during eighth grade and then begin the math curriculum for science majors at the university. This assistant chairman agreed to present his case to Jacob's school counselors, math teachers, and principal. He went to the meeting and laid out the plan for the committee, telling them exactly what he wanted for Jacob the following year: Let him zoom through his high school math, "and then we will take over from there."

"How could they refuse?" Jacob's mom asks. "One of the highest level people in the math department at the university had just told them they would accept Jacob into the program. It was an absolutely beautiful moment. This man had to travel in the middle of a school day, half an hour, to advocate for a boy he had met only once. He did this because he believed that if Jacob had been forced to remain in high school math only, he would have been extremely bored and probably would have hated math as a result."

Sometimes mentors simply appear when kids ask questions. Seven-year-old Jennifer has always been interested in photography. A few years ago she received a camera for Christmas, and she taught herself how to capture the images she wanted. Jennifer's family developed her film at a wholesale club's one-hour photo booth. The man behind the counter noticed the girl who came to pick up her own photos every week. This man, Larry, invited Jennifer to visit the booth on a Saturday morning to learn how the film was processed, developed, and printed. She did, and she marveled as the machines transformed negatives into photos. The next time she visited, Larry gave her a photography assignment. She took the required pictures and then they developed her results together the following week. Since then, Larry—who, it turns out, teaches photography at the local high school—has continued to tutor Jennifer in photography using her mom's 35-millimeter camera. Jennifer is thrilled with her new knowledge, which helped her earn a Girl Scout badge in photography. She loves learning about light and color and what she can make the lens and flash do. Not bad, says mom, Carolyn, and "all from the guy at the one-hour photo booth!"

Sometimes, parents and children spend more time seeking mentors. Susan, who teaches in gifted programs at three different schools, agrees with Barry Jekowsky's assessment that parents have to be the general contractors of their children's lives. "Time after time I've seen that the gifted students who have more fully realized talents are the ones who have parents who act as mentors," she says. "These parents not only love and care for their children, but also expose them to new areas of interest and new activities." Mentoring parents help children learn to research their projects, and they arrange meetings with professionals. They take the time to attend classes and events with their children, and seek out competitions or other challenges so their children can gauge their accomplishments.

Susan knows that mentors can especially help children in scientific and creative fields. Her daughter Allie is an accomplished writer who has won prizes for her broad portfolio, which includes everything from expository essays to an excerpt from a fantasy fiction novel. From a young age Allie has also campaigned to save a species of fox that lives near her hometown of Ventura, California. In 1999, Susan's husband, Don, who worked as an archaeologist at Channel Islands National Park, told her and Allie about a new program to help save the endangered foxes and feed the captive ones on San Miguel Island. Allie said she wanted to help, so through a wildlife biologist they arranged a trip to care for the foxes over Christmas. Allie enjoyed the work so much that she wanted to do more. They kept talking with the wildlife biologist, who set up meetings for Allie with the wildlife managers at the Santa Barbara Zoo. Soon, Allie started the Save Our Species student conservation group, which has continued to grow. She even got to make a presentation on the group's Save the Island Fox program to Jane Goodall, primatologist extraordinaire.

Susan helped her daughter find mentors through networking and personal contacts. She tried the same approach in order to find a mentor to help Allie with writing—a necessity, Susan says, because the children's writing classes in the area didn't match Allie's advanced abilities, and the adult one-day workshops didn't seem to be a good match, either. Cold calls to universities didn't go anywhere, nor did inquiries among bookstore owners or local children's book authors, but it turned out that one of Allie's favorite novelists had a sister who was a former teacher at Allie's school. Her school librarian had known that teacher, and eventually the match was made.

Finding the right writing mentor took Susan and Allie a year from start to finish. Some programs try to make those matches easier. The International Telementoring Program, formerly part of the Hewlett-Packard Corporation, sets students up with e-mail mentors who guide them through specific projects. The mentors themselves choose those they guide. More than eleven thousand children have participated in this program.

Some school districts even arrange mentoring relationships for highly gifted children. Tahlequah High School in Tahlequah, Oklahoma, matches students in the gifted and talented program with area professionals in medicine, law, and other fields. The Lincoln Public Schools district in Lincoln, Nebraska, matches highly gifted children with mentors who are paid by the school corporation to meet with the child up to five hours a week during the school day. Because the program is run by the school, it has bureaucratic requirements, such as a minimum college GPA for the mentors and mileage reimbursement rates. Still, the Lincoln Public Schools' investment affirms that schools have a responsibility to arrange an appropriate education for highly gifted kids—even when this means one-on-one instruction. About three hundred students qualify for mentoring, and about two hundred have enrolled in the program, according to supervisor Tom Hays. A highly gifted student bored with English class in Lincoln can skip the class and work with a creative-writing mentor instead.

■ **Patrons**

The Lincoln Public Schools pay mentors to tutor highly gifted students. The International Telementoring Program charges a small fee. Very resourceful parents can find inexpensive ways to meet their children's needs. But, in general, individual instruction in gifted children's areas of talent can be staggeringly expensive. Music lessons cost hundreds of dollars a semester; high-quality instruments retail for thousands. Mathematicians need tutors and college classes. Writers need summer retreats and correspondence courses. Scientists need access to labs. When appropriate public schools aren't available, parents may have to fork over $5,000, $10,000, or more for private schooling or give up a parent's income so a child can be homeschooled. Parenting is expensive enough as it is. Parenting a child with special needs is even more expensive. Some families can afford to nurture their children's talents, but others simply can't.

That's when patrons become necessary. Like the musical mentoring system, patronage has long and romantic roots. The Medicis in Florence encouraged, supported, and rewarded Renaissance geniuses for works that remain among the best in Western art. They also sponsored scientists and inventors such as Galileo. Pope Julius II himself sponsored Michelangelo. But patrons aren't needed only at the advanced levels of a craft. Highly gifted children need them, too, to ensure that there will be Galileos and Michelangelos in years to come.

A few years before we met the Giordano family, an anonymous patron helped save them from an educational disaster. The family's oldest son, Marc, had a voracious appetite to learn about everything around him. An aunt gave the family a map of the United States, and not knowing what to do with it, Marc's parents hung it by his bassinet. He would stare at the poster. The family ran a delicatessen and pizza shop in a Long Island commuter town. When Marc was a year old, they would put him in a crib in the window of the shop so they could keep an eye on him while they worked. He would sit there in the window and, to occupy himself, nibble bits of cheese into the shapes of the states. Before he was two he could recite the names of the states and their capitals. He liked to stare at a globe and soon learned to locate countries by name.

People started coming to see this strange little boy in the

window, and for a while he was a media star. A psychologist saw him on TV and insisted he be tested. Marc's parents agreed. He hit the ceiling of the assessment, so the psychologist could only tell them that his IQ was over 160—and that was a conservative estimate.

Soon the Giordano family started looking into where Marc would go to school. They went to the local elementary school to find out what could be done for this precocious little boy, but the meeting was a disaster from the start. The psychologist didn't trust his IQ scores, and others insinuated that his mom, Judy, was a stage mother who only thought she had a profoundly gifted child. It soon became clear that the local elementary school couldn't help them, and that put the family into a panic. Marc wanted to go to school, but where could he go?

The Giordano family heard about a place called the Long Island School for the Gifted (LISG), a private school not far from their home. LISG catered to children with IQs over 145 and understood the need to change the curriculum for students who required more challenges. The director had heard of Marc and invited his parents to take a look. But they couldn't afford the tuition for the next year, when Marc would be in kindergarten, and while the school offered some financial aid, it wasn't enough. So Judy kept him out of school for another year and tried to teach him herself. Marc raced through his work, exhausting the resources of the local library. Judy struggled to find lessons. Meanwhile, the family ate macaroni and cheese and hot dogs to save all the money they could. Aunts and uncles chipped in, and finally they scrounged up enough to pay the tuition at LISG for Marc's first grade year. The first day he came home beaming. "It's like being in heaven," Marc said. "The kids are like me."

Judy could see how much he was learning at LISG and how

much he loved to learn with friends who wanted to learn as much as he did. She knew he needed to stay there. But soon the family had various medical emergencies that wiped out the savings they had. They couldn't afford another year's tuition. Judy researched every scholarship she could find, but none helped children under age thirteen. They didn't know what to do. The tuition bill was coming due.

But then someone in Katonah, New York, heard about the family's plight. The minister of the donor's church sent Judy a check for $2,000 just in time. Now, several years later, Marc is still at LISG, learning more about the geographical and social studies topics that fascinate him. The family has since found other funds, but that one anonymous patron truly touched this child's life.

After we sold our software company in 1996, we decided to become patrons ourselves. We have found the experience of supporting bright young people as they develop their talents to be quite rewarding, particularly when we see what these young people can do. For instance, we started a Learning Partnership program at the University of Nevada at Reno to give middle and high school students the opportunity to do real research that challenges them and develops their scientific talents. The president of Nevada, Dr. John Lilley, helps us find mentors among the University's faculty. Dr. Jim Hager, superintendent of Washoe County Schools, helps us identify students from Reno schools who would benefit from this partnership. One high school student, Breanden, joined Professor Jesse Adams at Nevada to work on nanotechnology research. He proved himself during a trial month and now has signed on to work in the lab for at least a year. That wasn't a hard commitment to make— he's having "an amazing experience." "I'm learning about this brand-new field and breakthroughs of nanotechnology first-hand," he says. He's learning everything from microscopy to macro structures formed by nanotechnology principles and applications. He's learning math and science that he otherwise wouldn't see until college. Breanden spends fourteen to twenty-five hours a week doing research and will soon be listed as an assistant researcher on a major paper. Within the next year he hopes to be published as lead researcher on his own project. Someday, he wants to be a plastic surgeon and help advance that field.

We've been happy to help support Breanden, and we've been happy to help other students around the country with scholarships and funds for lessons and tutoring. But we can't help everyone. This country needs thousands of philanthropists to become patrons of gifted students. Prize money encourages kids to try hard things and stretch themselves to win recognition. Scholarships can mean the difference between a good school experience and a bad one. Even a small stipend for piano lessons can help grow an accomplished musician. It's amazing how far a small investment can go. Gifted kids are every bit as worthy a cause as museums and universities, and as we've seen again and again, investing in one talented child brings rewards far beyond what we originally imagined.

■ Stopgap Solutions

Teachers, mentors, and patrons can help find and polish rare gems from the quarries of American schools, but finding the right teachers, mentors, and patrons takes some luck and a lot of effort. It takes caring adults willing to invest hours of their time solely for the love of teaching. And while flexible, generous teachers are wonderful, in the normal school environment even these miracle workers can't work all the miracles needed.

When Monique's parents planned to move from New York City to the suburbs, they searched for the best school districts, based on published rankings, college acceptance rates, and the like. They knew that their eldest daughter was very smart. Still, "it never occurred to us that the public school would not meet her needs when we were moving to our 'highly rated' public school district," says mom, Priya. She and her husband, Derek, had come to the United States after growing up in Guyana. In Guyana, schools made a point of congregating the brightest students from all walks of life in order to use the country's limited educational resources to challenge these children. In Derek's and Priya's academically selective high schools, they met children of peasants and children of foreign diplomats. They valued this diversity and wanted to send their own children to public schools. "As immigrants to this great nation that Derek and I love dearly, how could we ever envision that our children could be underserved by the American educational system?" Priya asks.

The system did try to serve them. Every year they met with teachers and administrators to discuss Monique's needs. "Unfailingly, each teacher from first to fourth grade received us warmly," Priya says. "The first grade teacher produced individualized spelling lists each week of quite sophisticated words. The second grade teacher asked us if we could recommend any resources to help her teach Monique, and she immediately ordered *Teaching Gifted Kids in the Regular Classroom*. The third grade teacher worked with the gifted teacher to come up with independent research projects for Monique and a few other children in the classroom." The school suggested that Monique skip the rest of third grade and requested private testing to better understand the girl's needs. After Monique skipped a grade, the fourth grade teacher sent math home for her to review so she could make the transition smoothly. "They all returned phone calls promptly or sent home notes apprising us of the situation in class," Priya says.

Still, it wasn't enough. Monique was bored despite everyone's efforts. Eventually, Priya and her husband enrolled Monique in the Long Island School for the Gifted, just as Marc's parents did. "After we sent her to LISG," Priya says, "we realized that practically *all* her time in public school had been a waste. It was great to have caring teachers, but they are limited by a system that is superficial, by a lack of training, and by the political correctness of egalitarianism during the elementary and middle school years."

Now that Monique's little sister is also enrolled at LISG, Priya sees what Monique could have had there. "We can see how Maud's first grade reading class at LISG gets the kids to think critically and to analyze, compared with Monique's years in reading in the public school, just regurgitating facts. Maud does real science twice a week at LISG, while even in fifth grade in the public school Monique was doing science every three weeks or so. Monique said it was boring because she 'knew the stuff anyway.'"

Policy makers and education experts have been talking a lot recently about "leaving no child behind." In this new era of standards and assessment, Monique's old public school will be praised for its high test scores, and failing schools will be told to emulate its methods. But even this good school in a good district couldn't meet a highly gifted child's needs. The curriculum was broad, but not deep, the teachers helpful, but hampered by rules and too low expectations. The children at this school were mostly of above-average intelligence, but that didn't guarantee Monique the true peers she craved.

Monique and Maud's parents are well-educated profession-als who can afford the tuition at a school that does meet their children's needs and fills a gap even the best teachers and men-tors can't overcome alone. We are thrilled that they have this re-source available.

But what about families that can't afford to pay $10,000 per child per year? We can't just cross our fingers and hope that these children will find mentors or master teachers who will nurture their talents outside the school day, or patrons who will cover tuition for extra classes or a better school. Schools in this country should give all children a free and appropriate educa-tion. Until every gifted child can attend a school where the brightest are appropriately challenged in an environment with their intellectual peers, America can't claim that it's leaving no child behind.

Chapter 6

School Solutions:

"I Do Not See Boredom Here"

N O OUTSIDE SIGN identifies the Charter School of Wilmington, Delaware; the school budget never included funds to spruce up the building's facade. A taxi driver asked to drive there from the train station scratches his head as he winds through Wilmington's rundown neighborhoods. But he can find the old Wilmington High School, where the Charter School now occupies the top floor. The school shares the physical maladies of the building it inherited: ceiling tiles drip when it rains; floor tiles sport cracks. The shocking blue shade of many classroom walls speaks to the generation gap in styles since the last paint job; the black floors speak to someone's decision to hide decades of scuffs and dirt.

Yet the Charter School of Wilmington's success with gifted students shows in one parent's response to the annual survey: "My son wants to do well in school because it's cool to be smart. He wants to do as well as his friends."

Veteran principal Ronald Russo pushes the stack of surveys across his office table as he explains why so many highly gifted students keep praising his school. "The environment encourages students to higher achievement," he says. "I do not see boredom here."

Chartered in 1995 with start-up capital from a handful of Delaware businesses that wanted a math-and-science-focused public school to attract employees to the state, Charter (as the students call it) isn't officially academically selective. For its first three years every student who applied was admitted. But since more students now want to attend than the school has places for, the admissions director can choose students who have shown an interest in math and science. Consequently, many students could be considered gifted. Median test scores of the applicant pool hover around the 90th percentile.

Charter's philosophy is simple: The curriculum will challenge all students. When concentrated in one school, the brightest students will push each other to higher achievement than if scattered. Because so many of the students are high achievers, student culture will value the life of the mind. That culture will give gifted children a sense of belonging and accomplishment that many have never felt before.

Chintan is one of those students. Before he came to Charter, he was a bookish student at a middle school where it was not okay to be bookish. Students teased him for taking eighth grade math in seventh grade, but even the eighth grade math bored him. He had few people to discuss his interests with, and many were so actively hostile that they would knock the books from his hands as he walked down the hall. "Sometimes I wondered how I would make it through five more years of school," he says.

Then his parents found out about Charter. Chintan applied and was accepted. Even on the first day of orientation he found a different world, "a place where I fit in," he says. He took the most challenging classes he could find. His success in these classes made him a role model for other students rather than a target for bullying. Teachers encouraged his love of math. With their support for his research, he undertook a project a few years ago of replicating heart functions with nonlinear mathematics to predict and control the effect of a pacemaker and certain drugs on cardiac cells. The results won him national recognition. The science he learned at Charter helped him land a spot on the U.S. Physics Olympiad team. Although he has zoomed through multivariable calculus and discrete math, at Charter even Chintan has classes that stretch his mind. And he has peers who want to do the same. At Charter, "People who are enthusiastic about learning are praised instead of looked down upon," Chintan says. He doesn't need to hide his intelligence; he can nurture it and start a promising life as a scientist and mathematician whose work may someday shape these fields.

Going to Charter, Chintan says, changed his life. Instead of trying to survive school and endure an anti-intellectual culture, he is growing his mind. That is why gifted students need schools where they can be challenged to the extent of their abilities while surrounded by their intellectual peers. These peers do not need to be the same age. But without assurances for mental and personal growth, American schools will continue to be responsible for the tragedy of wasted talent and time.

When we visited Charter on a snowy February day, the school's nearly one thousand ninth to twelfth graders jostled one another in the hallways between classes like other students, but when we looked at the walls, we saw a difference. Here, bright yellow signs advertised a Learning Lunch. A local vaccine expert was giving a talk, and students could bring their lunches and listen. So many students showed up that the speaker was invited back to repeat her talk.

We know of no traditional high school where this would happen. Gifted students thrive best in a place like this where it does.

Charter's course offerings themselves accelerate students through college-preparatory math, science, and language arts, and allow students to specialize with offerings in discrete math, forensics, and biotechnology. The humanities offerings include electives in art history and English literature for students who want to pursue these topics. Many students choose Charter because it is the top high school in the state, not just because they are interested in math or science. Over the years the school has strengthened its humanities offerings for these kids.

Even though most of its students are gifted, Charter still believes in ability grouping. Entering students take a math and reading achievement test, which places them in one of three tracks, or "phases," as Principal Russo calls them. Students can test out of classes by taking a "challenge" exam; if they already know a course's content, they don't have to take the course. All students do a senior research project. Russo hires teachers who are committed to continuing their own education and to helping bright students absorb all they can. They earn no more than at other public schools, but the desire to be part of Charter's intellectual environment draws teachers with superb—and even superfluous—qualifications. A Spanish teacher has a Ph.D. in science. A biology teacher is a licensed chiropractor. Russo himself has degrees in physics, law, and business. He mentions a math teacher whose students prodded one another into finishing the assigned textbook early in the year, so the teacher found a more advanced textbook and kept teaching.

For this environment students flock from everywhere in the state of Delaware. One student, Russo says, commutes one hundred miles round trip each day. No matter: He can read or do homework on the bus. Jason, another Charter student, was homeschooled up until the eighth grade. Charter's scientific offerings impressed his parents so much that they put him in school there for ninth grade. The classes he took helped him design experiments to test whether a certain antibody could slow the growth of tumor cells. He conducted this cancer research over the summer at an area lab and is now pursuing a patent for his results. Jason also has courses at Charter that challenge him.

When we caught up with Jason and Chintan after they'd finished classes for the day, the only complaints they had about their school was the state of the building and that Delaware didn't have schools like Charter available for their whole kindergarten-to-twelve careers.

Both agree that at Charter "your number of AP classes is like your status." In addition to academics, Charter offers competitive sports teams, and when we were there, students pored over the posted list of parts assigned for the adjacent Cab Calloway School of the Arts' production of *Les Misérables,* which students at both schools could audition for. Charter has a prom, driver's ed, and all the trappings of high school. But here, high school also means a community of scholars. Elsewhere, Jason says, "Learning is subjugated to 'going to school.' At Charter it's the other way around." He recently did some outside reading that involved complex math that he didn't understand. He brought the article to a teacher after school, and she helped him figure it out.

Here, Chintan says, "There is competition for spots on the Math League and Science Olympiad teams instead of a lack of members. Topics dealing with math and science occasionally come up during conversations."

Russo has big plans for Charter. Since the state charter-school legislation frees him from the "traditional bureaucratic mentality," as long as he can find the money, he can make these dreams happen. He wants to expand the school to cover grades six to twelve, and he wants to bring in college professors from the University of Delaware to teach college credit classes to his students, so the most advanced can graduate with an associate degree. His board of directors wants a new building to match the high-quality academics, but parents and students understand that this isn't the most important part of the school. Charter would be Charter even in trailers as long as the school keeps bringing the state's most talented teachers and students together.

"It's enjoyable to be around people who love learning as much as you do," Jason says. "It challenges you to do better." It's not for everyone. "For some people the normal public school system works just fine," he says. But for many like Jason and Chintan it doesn't. For their sake this country needs a lot more schools like Charter.

■ Where Gifted Students Learn

Parents, teachers, mentors, and patrons can all help gifted children reach their potential, but as long as governments collect taxes to support universal compulsory schooling, public schools will remain the primary places where education in this country takes place. While schools do wonderful things such as introduce children to a common democratic culture and provide hubs for communities, as Jason says, *learning* shouldn't be subjugated to going to school. All children should learn to the extent of their abilities. When schools don't help children learn, the schools must change.

Since we became involved with gifted education, we've worked with many schools to find ways to nurture highly gifted students. We've also found schools such as the Charter School of Wilmington that already meet these children's needs. These schools have many things in common:

They group students by competency in each subject, not by age.

They do not make students study material they already know.

They change the curriculum to fit the child. Learning is a fixed goal; strategies are flexible. These schools will try anything to help children learn—including distance learning, independent study, mentoring, subject-matter acceleration, dual enrollment (letting students take classes at a middle school and high school at the same time, for instance)—to make sure they don't waste children's talents and time.

They offer competitions and talent searches so students can measure their knowledge against that of others.

They celebrate their high achievers' accomplishments.

They let students accelerate—either skip whole grades or go to different grades for individual subjects—if that is the best choice.

They recognize the special needs of gifted students, including career planning and counseling needs, and the need to explore favorite subjects in depth.

Teachers recognize the importance of nurturing talent, including their own, and continue their own education to make sure they meet the needs of all special learners.

Parents, administrators, and teachers all work together for the common goal of challenging children to the extent of their abilities.

School culture values intellectual discovery. Learning is considered exciting and a joy. Students encourage one another to accomplish more than they would on their own.

These strategies aren't rocket science, yet few schools have them in place. Instead, schools that claim to have gifted programs often shuffle gifted students into pull-out classes for just a few hours a week. Many secondary schools that claim to have gifted programs let students advance just a year in math and take modestly more challenging English classes, regardless of the child's ability.

And some schools don't even bother with that. "Our school spent more in time, energy, and money fighting an appropriate plan than it would have cost to implement a plan," says one mother, "all because 'we don't *do* gifted here.'"

From working with schools across the country, we know that the ideal solution for meeting the needs of gifted students is creating schools specifically for them, schools that support a student culture where it is acceptable to discuss one's ideas and projects at the lunch table. Even excellent and well-funded traditional schools lack this culture, and at most schools, meeting the needs of low-ability students keeps teachers from meeting those of high-ability students. Excellent teachers can satisfy both, but they won't have an easy time of it.

Any large district can create a magnet primary and a magnet secondary school for high-ability students. Smaller districts can combine to create such schools—the kids will travel for this opportunity. Any district can combine high-ability learners in self-contained classes, give them teachers trained to aim two to three years above grade level, and change the curriculum to challenge those who need more.

When people ask us what schools can do to help highly intelligent students reach their potential, we tell them that ability grouping of gifted students is the most important step. It will be a difficult battle to get districts to create such schools, especially in districts that are committed to the idea of local schools that group students by age, not ability. But even if the battle has only just started, we can still daydream about what kind of schools will best serve highly gifted children once they are liberated from the age-grade lockstep.

Several districts and states around the country have created high schools such as the Charter School of Wilmington for gifted students, but primary schools are just as important. A child whose love of learning is nurtured early will better weather the later storms of an anti-intellectual, least-common-denominator world. An ideal primary school for highly gifted children would structure the curriculum to fit the child's needs as she grows and learns. Children might have a coordinating teacher of a certain grade, but they could move freely back and forth between different grades for different subjects depending on the child's ability. Because all children would do this, most classes would contain children of many different ages—and that wouldn't be seen as strange. Teachers would assess children's progress periodically so that they could switch to another class whenever they exhausted the resources of the first.

Teachers would use a thematic approach. A broad concept such as "courage" could tie together *Huckleberry Finn* and the science that led to Galileo's run-in with the Inquisition. Children could delve as deeply into these themes as they were able. To help them, such a school would make searchable resources available, from the Internet to nearby research libraries' collections. Students could be assessed on their inquiries, on their ability to pose questions and answer them through higher-level thinking. Highly gifted children, like all children, need to learn reading, writing, and arithmetic, but these skills are means to an end, the further pursuit of knowledge, not an excuse to fill hour after dreary hour until the child finishes the primary grades. Highly gifted children learn these skills quickly because these skills help them learn more. They need schools that understand this desire to learn.

An ideal primary school would bring in experts in different fields to further feed students' curiosity. Such a school would understand that even gifted children show different levels of precocity and that what works for one won't always work for another. And such a school would not hold a certain number of grades sacred. When the child has exhausted a primary school's resources, whatever his age, it is time for him to move on.

Creating such schools would not cost more than miseducating gifted children in regular classrooms. Any decently sized school district can create such schools. And even the tiniest school system can accelerate a child until she is in a grade with students of similar intellectual ability; such a solution even saves money as children zoom through school.

All an appropriate education for the gifted child takes is a bit of political courage, the flexibility to try different options, and a conviction that all kids deserve to have their needs met. School districts that do not choose these solutions fail their gifted children. It is as simple as that.

■ "This School Will Save Some of These Kids' Lives"

In Muncie, Indiana, the Hoosier state has learned how not to fail its gifted children, at least for their last two years of high school. Every August, seniors at the public residential Indiana Academy for Science, Mathematics, and Humanities watch a certain giddiness come over the 150 new juniors when they arrive on the campus near Ball State University. Students discover the joy of throwing themselves into the mastery of difficult academic work while studying, socializing, eating, and living with other bright students. Unlike talent search summer programs, they don't have to leave after a few weeks to endure a dreary school year. This *is* the school year. What most gifted kids consider near paradise is suddenly home.

Laura visited the Indiana Academy as a prospective student after she missed two weeks of classes at her old high school because of illness. When she recovered, she returned to discover that her honors English class had just read out loud one hundred pages farther into a novel she had finished the first night it was assigned. The Utopian Literature class she visited at the Indiana Academy featured a discussion on the use of dream sequences and letter devices in fiction—and the students didn't snicker when she defined "epistolary." At her lunch table at the old school, students discussed who was not currently speaking to whom. Academy students gossiped, but they also debated political issues. The calculus teacher at her local high school puzzled through what to do once she exhausted the school's math resources that year. At the Indiana Academy a counselor suggested a sequence of math electives that could build on her calculus foundation. "Here," Laura told her mom during the car ride home, "teachers actually care what students *think*."

So she enrolled the following August and soon showed that same giddiness as her new classmates as she wandered all over the Rust Belt town—to the river with a guitar-playing crew, to the local coffee shop to chat—with new friends who liked being smart. She had to figure out how to budget her time. Her first semester's B's and C's showed her lack of study skills, but she soon learned how to ponder problems late at night and feel connections forge in her brain. "The Indiana Academy gave me my mind back," she says. Like Chintan at the Charter School of Wilmington, Laura couldn't imagine how she would have survived if she had stayed at her local high school.

Like Charter, the Academy offers students a curriculum that is both broad and deep. Students learn chemistry, botany, literature, and playwriting. Their social studies classes read the political theorists who influenced America's founders. Students study statistics, differential equations, and other math electives beyond calculus. They study Chinese or French, or take classes offered at nearby Ball State. They join the university's choirs and dance troupes, and they play on sports teams at the Burris Laboratory School, where the Academy holds classes. They learn to work for their grades. Friendly competition with their peers pushes them even further. The Academy welcomes young scholars from all different backgrounds and supports them as they live and learn together. "This school is one of the most forward-looking things the state has ever done," says Tracy Cross, the Academy's executive director.

Since former North Carolina governor James B. Hunt, Jr. proposed the first state-sponsored residential school for the gifted in 1978, thirteen states from Indiana to Texas have created similar institutions where bright kids can learn with their intellectual peers. Because these schools draw students from all over some large states, they live in dorms, often near a university campus.

Most such schools enroll only juniors and seniors. It's a matter of cost, says Cross. You either cut the student body or limit the years, and some people in states without long histories of boarding-school education don't want kids to leave home before age sixteen.

Most of these schools focus on math and science. The Indiana Academy incorporates the humanities as well and so brings in a more diverse group of kids. Students can specialize in a way that traditional public schools make difficult. Their teachers keep office hours, and students regularly inhabit their favorite teachers' offices for these informal salons.

The Academy's students have standard teenage angst-related problems. They chafe against strict rules put in place for liability reasons. Some sport bizarre clothes and hairstyles. "The ones who come to our school have chosen to give up things and to live in a less comfortable environment," Cross says. Many would never be "normal" anyway; however, "as a psychologist, I know this school will save some of these kids' lives," he says. There is pain in not using one's mind. At the Academy students will discover what it is like to receive an appropriate education, often for the first time.

Gifted students from Alaska to Florida deserve this opportunity as much as students in Indiana or North Carolina. All states should have such schools, and they should cover more than just two years. Providing room and board in addition to the regular per-student payment costs no more than what states spend on special education; gifted kids have special needs too. As a last resort, states can charge a fee for room and board and look to foundations for grants to subsidize families that are unable to cover the cost. But "too expensive" is no excuse. States have to pay to educate these students anyway; they may as well spend the money in a way that works.

For states considering residential high schools, Cross recommends locating near a university campus in order to tap its resources. Why spend limited high school funds on a research library when a university can provide this? In addition, colleges attract cultural events and allow the school to offer more advanced classes for students who need them.

Like Russo at the Charter School of Wilmington, Cross hires teachers who enjoy working with gifted teenagers and who are committed to continuing their own education. Teachers who love to learn inspire students who love to learn. Cross himself has taught classes and does research on gifted education. He never planned to be an administrator, but he has found a calling that does more for Indiana's brightest students than research would. "If we can't get excited about bettering the lives of these kids, then what are we about?" he asks.

States must also make sure that students know about their residential schools. Many high schools, fearful of losing the students they won't nurture but like to brag about, will not inform students about the opportunity. The Indiana Academy advertises. The school also broadcasts AP classes, lab instructions, and even field trips to satellite classes around the state for students who aren't willing or able to leave home.

These schools, as Cross says, can save lives, but the state benefits, too. The Academy meets the state's promise to truly educate highly gifted students, at least for two years. Some legislatures have created these schools because they hope to keep students in state for college, and about 60 percent do stay. But Cross thinks that's a misguided goal. If a student wants to go to Princeton, she won't change her mind because of the Academy and go to Indiana University. But maybe students will come back to the state. Quality schools attract quality workers who want the best possible education for their children. "These kids at the Academy will change the world," Cross says. "Coming here means we're enhancing the likelihood that they'll do that and improve conditions within the state and enhance the future of this country. There's no better reason for a state to set up a school than to develop the potential of its youth."

■ **Zooming Ahead**

Until all districts or states have schools such as the Charter School of Wilmington or the Indiana Academy for students of all ages, acceleration—skipping a grade when a child has already mastered that grade's content—is the best way to match highly gifted students with others of similar intellectual abilities. Learning is a sequential process. Highly gifted students move through these sequences more quickly than others. Accelerating them through school provides an appropriate education for their mental age, plus it's cost-effective: Eleven years of education costs less than thirteen.

When we started working with gifted children, we assumed that, given the constant funding crisis most districts experience, educators would embrace acceleration for the highly gifted. Yet we've learned that when it comes to skipping grades, fiscal prudence flies out the window. Nothing inspires more alarm among educators than the suggestion that a seven-year-old should become a fourth grader or a ten-year-old a high school sophomore or a fourteen-year-old a high school graduate.

"For some . . . acceleration as an educational option is simply out of the question," James Borland, a professor of gifted education once wrote. "These individuals seem to view the prospect of a child deviating from the one-grade-per-year lockstep not simply as a modification of a somewhat arbitrary administrative convenience but rather as a contravention of the laws of nature." Some see it as contravention of a higher law than that. As one gifted girl said, her school's attitude was that if God wanted her to be a ninth grader, He would have made her be born a year earlier.

Objections to acceleration boil down to two main lines of reasoning: The child will suffer social and emotional consequences, and she will have gaps in her knowledge. Even educators who are otherwise sympathetic to the needs of gifted students pose these arguments. Erika Rosa is assistant principal of the Virginia elementary school that Cathy, one of the children we've worked with, attends. Rosa says that "as a general rule of thumb, grade skips are not an option. Teachers are expected to differentiate lessons to meet the individual needs of all students. When discussing the possibility of a grade skip, my hesitation is the gaps that children may acquire in their learning."

Likewise, administrators at the Charter School of Wilmington shy away from letting students skip seventh or eighth grade in order to enroll in this school early.

We would never argue that acceleration is a good idea for all highly gifted children. Some lack the maturity to handle situations that older students encounter. Some highly gifted students are happy with children their own age, particularly if provided with advanced subject material. Some of the children we know use distance learning or software such as Stanford University's Education Program for Gifted Youth within their regular classrooms and in this way stay challenged without acceleration.

Yet too many schools lack the resources or willpower to make vast accommodations within a child's age grade. Most lack a school culture where teachers match the curriculum to the child. In these cases, acceleration shouldn't be seen as a controversial measure fraught with peril that failed for "one child" years ago; it should be seen as a way to keep real children from going crazy where they are.

Acceleration has been thoroughly studied and found effective. One recent metanalysis of twenty-six major long-term studies found that accelerated gifted students perform at levels well above nonaccelerated age peers of similar intelligence. These studies showed no social or emotional outcomes that led students or parents to see acceleration as a bad idea.

Researchers who specifically study the social aspects of acceleration find the same thing. In the early 1990s, gifted education expert Miraca Gross undertook a study of extremely gifted children who skipped two or more grades. She found that afterward these students' parents and teachers strongly believed that the children had wound up in the right place, both academically and socially. The students said they were more motivated. They felt less pressure to underachieve in order to be accepted. They enjoyed closer social relationships than they had before being accelerated.

Long-term studies of children who enter college early (and have skipped several grades along the way) also show positive academic results and more often than not, positive social results too. (Please see www.GeniusDenied.com for a more complete listing of these studies.) Both adults and children form friendships based on shared interests. When kept with their age mates, gifted students face a dilemma of choosing friendships with children who don't share their interests or pursuing work that interests them. Highly gifted girls often choose friends and so stunt their own minds. Boys tend to choose their interests, and so appear antisocial. When placed with older children, they don't have to choose. These friendships with older children are stronger than the ones gifted students made earlier. Occasionally awkward situations arise—being the last to get a driver's license, for instance, or not being able to work during the school year like one's friends because of labor laws—but gifted kids are great problem solvers. They adjust.

Although the research is impressive, it's the children we've worked with who have convinced us that we shouldn't fear acceleration. Not all children who have skipped grades have satisfactory outcomes, but about 90 percent of the ones we work with do. Most highly gifted students select older companions anyway when they have the chance to do so. Acceleration allows gifted students to pursue their careers earlier and hence saves them time. It doesn't require schools to provide a special curriculum, so all schools can use it. Most accelerated students do just as well as (if not better than) the older students in their classes. Students mature at different rates anyway, as a glance around any seventh grade classroom will show. Birth dates help administrators keep track of children, but they don't provide too much information about the needs of the highly gifted. (For specific research on acceleration see www.GeniusDenied.com.)

Despite the research, however, many otherwise sympathetic educators remain hostile to the idea of acceleration. We suspect that, like CEOs who are so invested in their companies that they can't see fundamental problems, even gifted coordinators and well-meaning teachers have bought into the idea that the entire kindergarten-to-twelve curriculum exists for a reason beyond filling time until the child is eighteen and legally able to enter the working world. Acceleration chips away at this foundation. Why thirteen years? Why not nine or seventeen?

So educators repeat their concerns about gaps, as if missing a forty-five-minute lesson on the different kinds of clouds or on how to make a cursive Q will somehow scar a child permanently. They fret about socialization, and they romanticize learning with one's age peers in a way that has no relation to real life. Our friends and colleagues aren't all the same age. If school is supposed to prepare children for the real world, spending 180 days a year for thirteen years with people you have little in common with beyond a birth date is no more effective than grouping children by height.

Yet these old ideas die hard. If parents want their children to accelerate, they need to know the research and how to address educators' concerns. The Iowa Acceleration Scale, developed by experts at the University of Iowa, features a useful tool to determine which grade would best suit a child. (For more details, please see www.GeniusDenied.com.) A child's score on this scale helps assure educators that no one is groping blindly in choosing the appropriate class. Some families have found it easier to time a grade skip to when the child would switch schools anyway or when the family is moving to a different district. The child should visit the proposed grade a few times to see if it is a good fit, and everyone should revisit the decision after a few weeks to make sure the child makes satisfactory progress. Parents must be willing to compromise and to help children with any gaps or social problems that arise from skipping grades.

But they also shouldn't sell this option short. Even some critics have come around. In his classic book *The Hurried Child*, published in 1981, child psychologist David Elkind warned that grade acceleration might deprive students of time and experience, and place unwarranted stress on them. Later, in 1988, Elkind clarified his view, endorsing acceleration when it addresses the educational needs of gifted children. "'Acceleration' is really the wrong word here," he says. "If it were correct we would have to say that a child who was retained was 'decelerated.' When an intellectually gifted child is promoted one or several grades, what has been accelerated? Surely not the child's level of intellectual development—that, after all, is the reason for his or her promotion! . . . What promotion does for intellectually gifted children is to make a better fit between the child's level of intellectual development and the curriculum."

Erika Rosa, the assistant principal, had her misgivings, but she firmly believes that education is about meeting the needs of the child. So she agreed to let young Cathy accelerate, and it worked well for her. For every child who is miserable after skipping a grade, there are a dozen others being made miserable by being left with their age peers. We do no service to these children by refusing to challenge our own untested beliefs to help them succeed.

■ Early College: "I Didn't Miss a Thing"

Acceleration can mean attending college early. Several colleges and universities sponsor programs for students who want to sail over high school.

Noshua Watson, a reporter with *Fortune* magazine, took the SAT through the University of Denver's talent search in sixth and eighth grades and went to summer programs at the University of Northern Colorado for three years. She loved her classes, and her parents loved the way she flourished. She discovered social skills and an enthusiasm for learning that her Boulder, Colorado, middle school was failing to nurture. She had few friends from school; she preferred the company of children from church or dance with whom she had more in common. She was always bookish, interested in academic endeavors, and frightfully bored. As one of very few African American students in her school, she had trouble relating to many of her classmates.

When she was in eighth grade, the Denver talent search program sent her a booklet of high school options. She had nudged her parents to send her to a boarding school, though with college for Noshua and her two younger sisters looming on the horizon, her parents shied away from the expense. But then her mother found listed in the brochure a program at Mary Baldwin College in Staunton, Virginia; it was an early–college entrance program for girls Noshua's age. Because the family planned to move to Maryland the next year anyway, Noshua visited Mary Baldwin with her parents. She toured the dorms, met others from the Program for the Exceptionally Gifted (PEG), and liked what she saw. She sent in her SAT scores (required to be as high as those of regular Mary Baldwin freshmen) and essays, and

PEG admitted her for what would have been her freshman year in high school, but instead became her freshman year of college.

PEG provided a peer group and support to help these young students succeed. Noshua took an extra semester of English to learn academic composition, analytical reading, and other skills that middle schools gloss over. She "telescoped" her remaining three years of high school math into one year so she could major in economics and take calculus her sophomore year. After a year or so, PEG students take regular classes for their majors at Mary Baldwin. "Going to college was the academic challenge I needed," Noshua says. And as for leaving home so young, "I was a pretty independent kid. I went because I was dying to get out of the house, and public school was just killing me." If her mind was grown up, she thought, why should she be somewhere where she had to ask permission to go to the bathroom?

Some PEG girls—particularly those not as self-sufficient as Noshua—had less happy outcomes. Some had family difficulties or could not handle the responsibility of living on their own. Some had trouble academically. And others, as at the Indiana Academy, had the "misfit" problem. Going to PEG is not the expected thing to do, so many of the girls are the maverick type. One of Noshua's classmates dropped out to manage a pizza shop rather than pursue more education. PEG certainly can't guarantee that these young women will immediately make socially useful contributions in an important field, but it does take these students' mental energy and put it to positive use. That by itself is an improvement over what many girls had at their previous schools.

Judith Shuey, head of PEG, notices that about her students.

"A lot of research shows that if gifted people aren't challenged, after a while they lose interest in challenging themselves," she says. They stop growing. They stop caring. At PEG many of these young women learn to care again.

For this, most PEG students don't mind sacrificing high school. After all, they can still go to events and mixers with high school kids in the area as long as they return to their dorms by curfew. Noshua went to a high school's prom. She asked friends questions about their school experiences. All in all, she says, "I didn't miss a thing."

Perhaps the toughest part is the moment of reckoning that all PEG students have when, as Noshua says, she realized she was seventeen, financially independent, and completely on her own. Now what? Most go to graduate school. Many transfer out of Mary Baldwin and repeat parts of college at the more selective schools they would have attended otherwise. Noshua pursued her master's degree at Stanford. "I don't regret not going to high school," she says. "I regret not spending more time in college as an undergrad." Still, Mary Baldwin provided a good liberal arts education, and Noshua liked the experience so much that her two younger sisters decided to attend Mary Baldwin through PEG as well.

Rudy Watson, Noshua's father, knows parents worry about sending their kids to college early. The Watson family chose PEG because it challenged their daughters *and* gave them a peer group with caring adults close by. "The concern was primarily due to their ages," he says. "I was not sure if each one was mature enough to make the proper choices, but the environment that they entered was nurturing enough to allow them to learn and to allow me to feel comfortable."

Watson advises other families considering such programs to make sure that "both the child and the parents are ready. This means emotionally as well as intellectually. Look for the best fit based upon the interests and personality of the student." This advice works for parents of high school seniors, too.

PEG is part of a small constellation of early entrance programs across the country. Simon's Rock College at Bard, where Rachel from Chapter 1 landed, enrolls only younger students (usually age fifteen or sixteen) and tailors the whole college experience to them.

Other early-entrance programs do not require students to leave home. Gifted-education expert Nancy Robinson and her late husband, Halbert, started the Early Entrance Program for young commuter students at the University of Washington because of their belief that "kids should stretch a bit to learn," she says. Younger students spend one year in a transition school where they condense much of the high school curriculum into a few months. By spring quarter they take one college course, and then they enroll as full-time students the next year. A substantial number land in the university's honors program. The Early Entrance Program attracts students who are bright but also mature and able to handle themselves in adult situations. Students who believe that "nothing at high school can compete with what they could do at the university," Robinson says.

Like PEG, it doesn't always work. "When it's a good fit, it's a very good marriage. When it's not, it's not," she says. "There's not a lot of in-between." Some students regret giving up parts of high school; others regret not going to Ivy League colleges. But others say they are glad they made that choice. Many would go to the University of Washington anyway, just several years later. And once students show they can cover the whole high school curriculum in a few months, it begs the question why they'd need all four years. Without the early-college program, "they would laze their way through high school," Robinson says.

"Some proportion would really turn off. Some would be okay, but not going at the pace they could." And while early college may require giving up certain things, "for a kid who doesn't fit the cookie-cutter mold, there is no perfect world," she says. "Life will be a series of compromises."

Colleen Harsin, who works with us at the Davidson Institute and has helped many young people consider early college, agrees. "If the choice is to remain with age peers and not have access to an appropriate education or access to a more appropriate education with older students, most students prefer the latter," she says. "They really didn't have a peer group with their age mates anyway."

But how much nicer not to face an either/or dilemma. This, Harsin says, is the beauty of early-entrance programs that truly give students a peer group—those of similar intelligence who are at the same stage of life. "The students have a better chance of having it all. While social and emotional variables cannot be ignored, they are often forced to take a backseat" to learning variables, she says. Early–college entrance programs, magnet schools, and residential schools for the gifted can give students the best of both worlds. (For specific schooling information, see www.GeniusDenied.com.)

Of course, many of the children we've worked with attend college early on their own, even without special programs. They simply enroll as full-time students in local universities, attend a few classes as part-time students, or audit ones that interest them as part of homeschooling. In none of the twenty or so cases we've followed has the student been overwhelmed by the experience. In fact, the only complaints we hear are about university or state regulations that keep these children from enrolling in more classes or enrolling outside the auspices of a sponsoring primary or secondary school.

Eight-year-old Kevin has been taking classes at a local university for a few semesters now. He was once a student in a normal elementary school and loved his friends, but he would come home crying because he was so bored. He got in trouble for switching his addition problems to multiplication and exponential functions. Eventually his mom, Rebecca, took him out of school. Kevin heard about another student who had taken college classes quite young, so he begged to try it. Rebecca relented and decided she may as well find out what he could do. Kevin's old school signed off on the idea, so the college admitted him. He took an astronomy class provisionally until he scored a 96 on the first test. Later he signed up for an earth-science class with a professor who was quite understanding and interested in helping this boy learn. Kevin enjoys interacting with the "big kids"—in part because he's fine with being different. His older brother has Down syndrome, so he knows that being different is okay and "that not everyone's going to treat him the same way." Rebecca says. He's done well taking math and music classes. Rebecca steers clear of literature classes because of the mature material involved. Early college works for this family because they don't treat it as a big deal. When we talked to them recently, they were considering a break during the next term so Kevin would have time for other things. They know the resource will be available when they need it again.

■ Schooling Children Who Don't Fit the Cookie-Cutter Mold

If schools and states aren't willing to create schools for the gifted or allow for grade skipping, the least they can do for highly gifted children and their families is make homeschooling easy and well supported. About a dozen states, including Pennsylvania, Alaska, and Arizona, offer cyber charter schools that support homeschooling families with curricula, knowledgeable advisors, and social opportunities. States have a variety of regulations on homeschooling, but more regulation doesn't raise student test scores. Homeschooled children in general do as well or better than their conventionally schooled peers.

Some of the families we've worked with are avid homeschoolers who have always wanted to teach their own children. One parent even suggests that we should see homeschooling as the norm, with traditional schools as the default option available if home learning doesn't work out. Many families, however, are more reluctant homeschoolers. They homeschool because they can't find appropriate schools. Some school officials even agree with the choice. "I have been struck by the responses I have gotten to our decision to homeschool from state-level educators here in Massachusetts," Sharon, a mom we have worked with, says. "All have the attitude of 'Great! You won't regret it! It's the best plan for your kids!' All the while they miss my point: I do not want to homeschool my kids. I do it because their system so fails my kids as to be harmful to them. And I want them to fix it, to see their responsibility to all students, even smart ones."

Some parents homeschool these "smart ones" because their children beg them to. Paul asked his parents to take him out of school because he was sick of being bullied for his bookishness and sick of being bored. His parents, who were tired of seeing their son's zeal for learning squelched, finally agreed.

Leslie's family, too, began homeschooling reluctantly. Leslie began her formal education at age two in a small church day school near her family's Texas home. The first day, Leslie showed the teacher she could read her name. She knew all her colors and began reading information off the wall. The teacher said, "Now, Miss Leslie, what are we going to teach you?"

School continued like this. Leslie's family enrolled her in a private elementary school in San Antonio, assuming it would be better than the local elementary school. But they soon learned that the school would not make any accommodations for Leslie's ability to work beyond her grade level. By the end of second grade Leslie was severely depressed, so her parents pulled her out. "We still deal with the repercussions and emotional scars brought on by leaving her for too long in an unsuitable academic setting," her mom says.

They found another kindergarten-to-eight private school that was willing to let her accelerate. She spent three years there. Although she wasn't challenged to the extent of her ability, she did have some understanding teachers who helped her learn to love learning again. She completed all the work through eighth grade and some of ninth grade by age ten. Her parents considered leaving her there for the social aspect, but two of her best friends decided to change schools, and then officials said they couldn't promise Leslie an advanced curriculum because she'd exhausted the school's resources. The family looked at high schools in the area, but couldn't find one that would place her in an appropriate grade. Some local universities, however, were willing to find a spot. Leslie sat in on classes and liked the college students' maturity level. Then she got her hands on Grace Llewelyn's *Teenage Liberation Handbook* (which advocates quitting school and getting "a real life and education") and asked to be homeschooled in the other subjects. She decided her primary school had no more to offer her.

The family gave the idea of homeschooling a lot of thought. "My husband and I were still hesitant to homeschool because we thought we would never be able to provide her with an appropriate education, and we were concerned about socialization," her mom says. "We finally decided to give it a try for a semester, along with a few college classes."

Leslie did exceptionally well that first semester. She was self-motivated and excited about learning. She grew more confident of her abilities because she was accepted by her classmates at the university and appreciated by her professors. Several recently wrote letters of recommendation for Leslie for a summer program. She takes distance-learning courses through programs for high school students and has joined a fencing club and a children's chorus. She tutors twice a week at the local elementary school. She's still happy about the decision to homeschool, and her mom and dad have become more comfortable with the idea too.

We're glad that this worked out for their family. Indeed, most of the families who have tried homeschooling enjoy it as well. But it's not for everyone. Parents such as Leslie's pay taxes to support their states' schools. Families shouldn't have to homeschool to give their children an education that challenges them to the extent of their abilities. And it would be nice for these students to have true peers as well.

We asked several homeschooling families recently what it would take to get them back in school. This isn't an idle question; moms like Sharon who don't want to homeschool have looked far and wide for these characteristics in schools, and many are willing to move to find them. Jason's family stopped homeschooling once they found the Charter School of Wilmington.

Catherine searched for schools in six different states and didn't find any that were willing to accommodate her highly gifted son. "The best answer I can give you is that a school

would have to have more flexible, permeable boundaries between grades to permit children—*all* children, not just the
highly gifted ones in which the problem is most acute—to do
the work they are demonstrably capable of doing *because* they
have demonstrated they can do it," she says.

Now she and her musician husband schedule their lives so
that someone can homeschool their son. "The problem with
schools is that they are institutions which must, for all kinds of
good reasons, sort children by some attribute or other, and
because the default attribute is chronological age, that does children performing wildly outside the norm for their age a considerable disservice," Catherine says. She was able to take her son
out of school because her job and her husband's job were both
flexible enough that they could teach the boy at home. Many
families don't have that option. What are schools doing for
them?

To receive an appropriate education, a child who doesn't fit
the age-grade cookie cutter can move to the appropriate grade or
have appropriate work moved to him. Neither is very hard to do.
"If schools were not constructed to fit curricula to chronology,
folks like us would be able to hack the school system," Catherine says.

The Charter School of Wilmington and a few other innovative institutions have helped families like hers find an appropriate education. America needs many more schools like these, but
these islands of excellence will remain few and far between
until the nation as a whole recognizes the cost of squandering
its brightest students' talents and time.

Chapter 7

Raising the Ceiling and the Floor

OVER THE YEARS, researchers have asked all kinds of questions about highly intelligent children: What kind of education do they need? Does acceleration work? What happens when their abilities aren't nurtured? In 1985 one researcher, Judy Galbraith, posed a novel question: How do gifted children themselves feel about being gifted?

She found, as we have, that young students complained that being gifted resulted in boredom, frustration, and occasional teasing. But their first gripe, confirmed in a follow-up study six years later, sums up the problem of educating high-ability students in this country as much as anything else: "No one explains what being gifted is all about," they said. "It's kept a big secret."

Little good comes from finding and labeling the country's brightest children if nothing happens other than the students receiving a few hours of enrichment a week. Whatever the school calls it, children in the gifted program know they are somehow different, but if they aren't challenged, then the whole mechanism makes no sense. These days the first children to experience full-scale gifted education in its often ineffective form have reached their mid-thirties. They liked the games and puzzles their pull-out programs provided, but many have different thoughts now as they realize that getting a label and taking a class on mythology won't make life any easier. Outside school the rules change. Being gifted can't substitute for knowing how to work hard and knowing how to take risks. Being gifted doesn't stop anyone from getting bogged down in middle management, from having to leap through hoops to gain tenure, from missing the big breaks necessary for an artistic career. Gifted students can coast through school with many honors and much talk of their potential, and still not do a blessed thing with themselves afterward. Some of the grown-up gifted children we've talked to are facing these obstacles and wonder whether their high IQs demonstrated anything beyond an ability to do well on tests.

We can't blame them for their confusion. The country as a whole hasn't made up its mind about gifted education. Educators and policy makers balance so precariously between concerns about equity and a desire for excellence that no one has made a compelling case for why nurturing the country's brightest students should land at the top of the educational to-do list. Every ten years or so, interested parties discover a crisis and issue a proclamation. In 1972, the Marland report brought the issue of gifted education into the national conversation and urged schools to nurture talent in many fields. The 1983 report "A Nation at Risk" warned that children were being dulled into complacency, and no one cared about the needs of high achievers. In 1993, "A Case for Developing America's Talent" said the same thing but failed to make any bold recommendations. Now another decade has passed, and we are still talking about standards, with the No Child Left Behind Act calling for tough measures to make sure that failing schools at least minimally educate all children. But the act contains no incentives for schools to educate children beyond proficiency for any particular grade level. We are still committed only to raising the lowest common denominator. The ceiling hasn't moved at all. If anything, it has fallen a few inches.

"The problem is not the pursuit of equality as such but the bias against excellence that has accompanied it," Professor Daniel Singal wrote in the *Atlantic Monthly* in 1991 about the "other crisis" in American education. We haven't seen anything in the intervening decade that has changed the picture. For a nation that likes to be the best in everything, we are awfully ambivalent about intellectual achievement. The regular school curriculum matches the needs of 50 percent or so of children. It will be too difficult for a quarter of students and too easy for the other quarter. Those in the very low percentiles are protected by laws requiring schools to meet their needs. The top percentiles, where the disconnect is worst, are on their own in trying to carve out an optimal match. Our anti-intellectual culture tries to dumb down these bright students. An obsession with everyone doing the same thing leads to inequality for students who have different needs from the norm. Both lead to gifted education becoming the "big secret" that students in the 1985 study griped about. We give these children some special treatment, enough to make them feel strange when they return to their regular classrooms, but rarely the kind that matters. We don't tell them what it's about. We halfheartedly call different classes the "Apples" group and the "Oranges" group rather than the different levels that children secretly know they represent.

America's ambivalence about talent leads to schools and society asking less and less of bright children, so over time they develop their talents less and less, and shrink into a shadow of the people they could be. This is genius denied.

As we've tried to show in this book, this tragedy has a face. Kids who love to learn discover that their gifts only make them miserable. But it also has a solution, and we've tried to show that too. This country will nurture genius when we stand up straight and say without apologizing that we need to nurture bright children—not only because it is the humane thing to do for their sake, but because these children are a national resource. Intelligence doesn't just mean doing well on tests. It's a measure of one's capacity to learn and solve problems. America's economy isn't labor-driven anymore; our brain reserves matter more than strong backs or how much coal or iron we have sitting around. A high IQ won't guarantee that a child grows up to be a productive adult, but a high IQ coupled with a challenging education and intellectual peers greatly increases the chances.

We'd be appalled at any agricultural policy that let food spoil in silos while people around the world were hungry. Failing to develop the talents of America's brightest students while they are young enough to stretch and grow their brains is no different. Since we know how much better gifted students learn in accelerated classes and how much they need intellectual peers, failing to provide an educational system committed to meeting these needs is like locking that silo door. Squandering resources does nothing to advance equality. Nurturing talent is not a zero sum game. In an era of constant change, those who can find and solve problems create positive benefits for everyone. Companies allocate resources more efficiently, inventions make life easier, and innovative solutions allow schools to stamp out the mediocrity that is plaguing too many classrooms in this country.

On some level most people know this. Americans value equality, but we'd like to have excellence, too. The two are not incompatible. This country has always dared to dream big. We can have both.

■ Achieving Excellence and Equity

Combining excellence and equity in education means a commitment to the idea that all children deserve to learn. All children deserve an education that challenges them to the extent of their abilities; this includes children who have been left behind and children who want to surge ahead. All too often, time is the constant and learning is the variable. At the average American school, children will sit at their desks for six hours a day, 180 days a year, for thirteen years, whether they learn anything besides habits of obedience or not. When a child is told she can't learn algebra in fifth grade because then "what will she do next year? And the next?" then time has replaced learning as the master. Children learn at different paces, but learning should be the constant.

Parents, teachers, schools, education officials, and legislatures can all help stop the waste of time and talent that makes school inequitable for highly intelligent children and keeps children from the excellence they can achieve.

When parents ask us what is the most important thing they can do to nurture their highly gifted children, we tell them that support and belief in these children's abilities both go a long way. Marie Capurro, who works with us as the Director of Programs and Services at the Davidson Institute, says, "Parents need to create a supportive home environment where children are loved and accepted for who they are, not for what other people think they should be. They should focus on their children's strengths and encourage them to do their best, not be the best." They need not push; more likely their children will pull them along, and parents need to be prepared for the ride and the speed bumps they encounter along the way. Many people insist that highly gifted children should fit into a mold of what is normal for a particular age, but parents need to realize that their children will never be "normal" and that they need a safe, secure home environment where that is okay, even if the neighbors roll their eyes.

Parents also need to realize that precocious children are by definition exceptional, and raising any exceptional child is a challenge. The child will demand much of the parent's time and attention. Raising exceptional children can be expensive, particularly when schools don't meet their needs. Few support systems exist for parents of highly gifted children and the children themselves. Most schools are not aware of the educational needs of highly gifted children, so parents have to advocate for their education even if that means being labeled "pushy." Sometimes high-ability children can fend for themselves, but other times they can't. Parents need to recognize when a child isn't challenged and work with school personnel to find a solution.

Educators also play an important role in nurturing genius. Good teachers learn to recognize common characteristics of gifted children in their classrooms and plan an appropriate education. They lobby their schools to be flexible with these children, and they create classes or programs that meet their needs. They foster an educational climate where intellectual inquiry is celebrated, and they insist that learning be the primary goal of school. If schools want to celebrate high achievement at graduation, they have to start in the early years by providing a learning environment where children can excel to the extent of their abilities without being teased or bullied or discriminated against because they are smart.

Good teachers and schools also see no point in making a child "relearn" what she already knows. They pretest their students at the beginning of each course to determine if students are already proficient in the material. They understand that seat-time requirements for diplomas and moving to the next grade benefit no one. Some districts offer the intriguing option of "credit by examination": If a child can pass the final exam for a class in the first week, no one gains by keeping him in the classroom for the whole year. The child wastes his time, and taxpayers waste their money. It is better to give the child credit and let him move on. Squandering resources isn't fair, and it isn't equality.

Schools and school districts pledged to equality also need to commit to creating schools and accelerated programs for their gifted students in order to provide them—as they do all other children—with an education that meets their needs. Teachers learn about meeting the needs of other exceptional students; they should receive training in meeting the needs of high-ability students too. All states should create guidelines for identification of these students. Most of the families we've worked with discovered their children's intelligence by arranging for IQ testing themselves. Schools need this information, too, and should be the ones doing the testing. Discovering a child's intelligence shouldn't depend on parents knowing how to work the system.

Schools should screen all students. Gifted children come from all races, income levels, and family situations. Often the brightest child is not the one raising her hand and blindly following the teacher's instructions. Schools should group children by competency level for instruction and monitor their progress to know which group best suits each child's needs. Schools that truly care about learning pretest, check, and evaluate the students' progress to ensure that no one is floundering or wasting time.

Likewise, schools that care about learning know gifted programs exist in order to help children learn, not to satisfy bureaucratic conditions or mollify parents with enrichment programs that more closely resemble indoor camp than school. We've heard ridiculous stories of high-ability children who moved to a district after the grade in which the district screens for gifted programs, so they weren't allowed to participate. We've heard stories of districts that refuse to provide any accommodation before third grade because they "don't do gifted" until then. Again, learning should be the constant, not time. The curriculum should always match the child and should change depending on need.

Districts and states can use many means of assessing children's capabilities. Talent searches, for instance, can find exceptional potential among middle schoolers and can give schools and districts better information for making secondary school choices. Few schools use these talent search scores or take advantage of the resources that talent search programs at various universities can provide. Schools that care about learning should.

Identifying these children does nothing if accommodations don't follow. Schools and parents need to collaborate to produce plans for matching highly gifted children with an appropriate academic curriculum. "Ninety minutes of pull-out a week" as a blanket accommodation for all gifted children isn't appropriate. Modifications can begin in the regular classroom but can't stop there. Schools and districts can provide multiple options, including independent studies, acceleration in different subjects or whole grades, distance-learning courses, dual enrollment in multiple levels of school (such as middle school and high school), Advanced Placement courses, mentorships with experts in the field, or, best of all, schools set up specifically for these students' needs. New charter-school laws hold promise for creating more places like the Charter School of Wilmington as well as elementary and middle schools that meet the same need. States can create residential high schools for the gifted and thereby invest in a crop of future leaders. But even regular schools can meet many of the academic needs of gifted children if these schools are flexible and use distance learning, grade skipping, and simultaneous enrollment in different levels of classes to help children learn. The particular details matter less than a commitment to creating rich learning environments that encourage high-ability students to develop their potential. True equality means all high-ability students have a chance to do these things.

Policy makers also have a role to play in helping gifted children achieve their potential. Some in the gifted-education community believe that children whose IQs are several standard deviations above the norm deserve the same sort of federal protection for an appropriate education that other exceptional children are entitled to. In the long run, such a measure might ensure that gifted children receive the education they deserve. However, we are wary of pushing for federal entitlement laws that have little chance of being passed. Disabled children deserve a share of the nation's educational resources under the Individuals with Disabilities Education Act, but following this federal mandate has caused some districts to spend themselves into poverty to meet the needs of these exceptional students. States and school districts will likely block a similar federal mandate for gifted children by claiming it is too expensive.

We believe the needs of gifted students are best addressed at state and local levels. State legislatures and districts should remove the obstacles that keep gifted children from receiving an appropriate education and should recognize that gifted children learn differently and have distinct educational needs. The state of Idaho, for instance, mandates that gifted students will have "the right to an appropriate education that provides educational interventions which sustain challenge and ensure continued growth within the public school system." The Boise schools state that their gifted program is "not provided as an honor nor a reward, but as an educational intervention for students who need it." Other states should follow Idaho's example. Policies that keep gifted children from learning all they can do not advance equity or excellence and deserve to be scrapped.

States, for instance, can protect children from age discrimination. No school should receive public funds if it refuses to provide a student with an appropriate education solely because of his or her age. If an eighth grader needs eleventh grade work, that district needs to make it happen or it should risk the same penalties it would incur for other forms of discrimination. The same applies to public colleges and universities. As long as a student meets the criteria for admission, age should not bar her from enrollment, scholarships, or financial aid. Public colleges and universities exist to serve the people of their respective states. When they discriminate against qualified people on the basis of race, religion, disability, or age, they break that compact and no longer deserve public support.

Currently, age restrictions reach deep into education for no better reason than to enforce the age-grade lockstep. For instance, in the absence of a high school diploma, some community colleges request a General Equivalency Diploma (GED) for enrollment. Financial aid programs and scholarships often require a GED. But in many states students must be sixteen, seventeen, or even eighteen to take this test. States have these regulations to keep children enrolled in school as long as possible. But gifted children aren't "dropping out"—most will go on to seek more education. If a child wants to forgo high school and go directly to college, she should be able to prove her competency on these tests and on high school exit exams where they are required, at whatever age she can. States can revise credit requirements for diplomas so highly gifted students who are already familiar with the material taught in many of these classes need not waste years to prove they are educated.

States should appropriate funds for identifying and serving gifted children; mandates do little if they aren't backed up with cash. Federal matching funds can induce states to find room in their budgets for gifted children. Legislatures can change education codes that require services for gifted students to supplement the curriculum and so breed pull-out enrichment classes instead of the accelerated coursework these students truly need. States and the federal government can evaluate schools based not just on the percentage of students who pass the state's standardized tests but also on whether parents and students are satisfied with how much children are learning. A school where a highly gifted student consistently scores in the 99th percentile but suffers through hours of boredom in class cannot claim it is leaving no child behind. State legislatures can make sure districts have the flexibility to meet all children's needs, and then they can reward schools that do just that.

We have seen what good, flexible schools can do. We have also seen how gifted children flourish in environments where they learn from others who love to learn, and learn alongside others who share their drive. We've seen what teachers, patrons, and mentors can do to nurture talent. We've seen what happens when children's minds soar as they are challenged to think. Our nation needs all the intellectual talent it can get. Society has too many problems to crush these children's intellects and keep them from becoming all they can be. The only reason educators, districts, and states get away with letting highly gifted kids be frustrated in school is that we have not made it clear that intelligence matters. But it does matter in every business decision made, every judicial decision cast, every public policy proposed, every disease diagnosed, every novel written, and every song composed.

We know children's intellectual accomplishments may never seem as sacred to the American experience as Friday night football games, but when these children grow up, their contributions to the pursuit of truth will last on the record books longer than any 11-2 season. Schools can celebrate academic achievement. Everyone from presidents to business leaders to clergy can condemn anti-intellectualism and expose the squandering of children's minds for the sin it is. Policy makers can worry as much about the children several standard deviations above the norm as they do about those below it. Journalists can follow student projects and make stars of the brainy as much as the brawny. Even Hollywood can make movies where intelligent people solve problems by using their heads—and it's considered cool. We've seen cities where gleaming stadiums rise courtesy of taxpayer money, while libraries can't stay open more than five days a week or purchase more than one copy of a book. For many bright children who can't afford dozens of new books of their own, these resources are the difference between discovering a different world and accepting the mindless world on TV. Nurturing genius means that the country's priorities have to change.

We believe that, over time, they will. As society becomes more complex, its challenges do, too. In a troubled and connected world, bright minds become even more of an asset. When Americans care enough about a problem, they solve it. We went to the moon. We can cultivate our Einsteins, too.

■ "Not All Kids Have to Be the Same"

A ten-year-old boy we know named Daniel wrote a paper recently on how Einstein's work expanded on that of Sir Isaac Newton. At the end he said that we won't have a homegrown Einstein in the near future "because the schools don't want one."

For a long time Daniel knew *his* schools didn't want one. He lives in eastern Tennessee with his adoptive mom, Tina, a social worker who is raising the child by herself. Tina thought Daniel seemed like a bright little boy, albeit a defiant one, but she didn't know how bright. Preschool had been a disaster. He landed in time-out a lot. Tina took him to a doctor for evaluation. The diagnosis came back—not ADHD (attention-deficit/hyperactive disorder), the pediatrician said. He was simply one of the most gifted children he'd ever seen. All that untamed mental energy was making this little boy lash out.

Daniel started school at the regular age. No one could figure out what to do with him. He had taught himself how to read, but that didn't change the work he was given. He wanted to check out a book on chemistry from the school library, but since it wasn't declared at his level, the librarian wouldn't let him. He came home with a reader filled with three months' worth of assignments. Daniel zipped through them in a night, so Tina initialed the assignments he completed, as the instructions told parents to do. The next day the reader came home with her initials whited out and a note saying: "Must stay with class." Daniel figured out multiplication ("It's a quicker way to add") and landed in the school's gifted program, but all that meant was forty-five minutes a week in a pull-out program. He still couldn't do things that interested him. He loved to read about science, and he desperately wanted to visit a lab with the older gifted children. But because his younger class wasn't ready, the teacher said that would be out of the question. Meanwhile, Tina met with school officials a dozen times during the fall of Daniel's first grade year to discuss why he was climbing the walls and getting into mischief in the long stretches of time after he finished his work before anyone else did.

Halfway through the year, the school finally moved him to second grade for a thirty-day trial. Daniel knew he was being watched. The pressure made him nervous, but he earned mostly A's on his assignments. As soon as he learned he would stay in the class, the anxiety disappeared. He became a mild-mannered child and finished the year in peace.

He moved to a magnet school for third grade. Halfway through the year he needed another grade skip. The school wouldn't budge. Tina retained an attorney, and she and the school compromised on a combination fourth and fifth grade placement the next year, with the understanding that Daniel could do higher-level work if he showed his teachers he was capable of it. Daniel worked diligently to prove he could, despite the mindlessness of the curriculum. He pored over chemistry books at night, while at school they learned about the scientific method by eating a brownie. ("Observe—how many chunks of chocolate? Hypothesis: The brownie will taste good.") He was very excited one night because the teacher announced they would do actual experiments the next day, but the next day he came home crushed. All they had done was pour water on trays representing different landforms. He asked for more challenging books, more challenging math. It never happened. He took this very seriously. What wasn't he doing right? Nine weeks into the school year he became so frustrated that his unused mental energy started eating into his body. He had to go on ulcer medication. Eventually, Tina homeschooled him for a few weeks while he recovered.

In February of that year he landed in a kindergarten-to-twelve magnet school, so in theory he could work as far ahead as he wanted with children of many different grades. That didn't happen, either. His base placement was in sixth grade. The teacher didn't like the idea of such a radically accelerated child joining her class. Daniel did fine with the work, but when things went wrong, it was always blamed on his age. Another parent called Tina to inform her just how hostile the class was becoming to her son, but Tina could tell from Daniel. He started getting sick again. He had such bad headaches that he landed in the emergency room for codeine. After the second trip Tina brought an attorney to meet with district officials again. She asked for homebound instruction. The district agreed, and Daniel learned at home for the rest of the year with a teacher visiting twice a week.

When this cured the headaches better than codeine, everyone figured out what was going on. The district sent a psychologist to give Daniel an intelligence test and to do an Iowa Acceleration Scale screening. His score put the boy, then nine years old, at a junior high level of intellectual development. For the next year district officials told Tina to pick a school she thought would work best. Originally she looked at the city's "best" middle school—one in a nice neighborhood that had a gleaming academic reputation—but when administrators there claimed no flexibility for making school work for Daniel, she settled on their zoned middle school. That school's students didn't have many of the same advantages, but from the beginning, administrators and teachers shared with Tina the attitude that "you don't have to stress over the little things. Not all kids have to be the same," she says. This school showed Daniel the whole course schedule and let him choose whichever sixth, seventh, and eighth grade classes he wanted. The gifted teacher in particular understood the boy. Daniel chose to stay in that man's classes for three hours a day. They would talk about Daniel's ideas. The teacher guided him through projects to develop these thoughts further.

He noticed Daniel's interest in chemistry, for instance, and encouraged him to do a science project in that field. So Daniel designed a Yu-Gi-Oh! card game based on the periodic table. He called the game ChemCraft and used it to test a hypothesis he had been told when he wanted to check out books from the library and visit a lab: "Can you be too young for chemistry?" He visited a fourth grade class and tested these students on their chemical knowledge. He led them in the Yu-Gi-Oh! game for a while, then tested them again. The children increased their knowledge and wanted to play more, to learn about valence and other concepts that he'd designed more card packs to introduce. Daniel left the class with a new respect for teachers, but also beaming because he had grabbed these children's attention and taught them something they didn't know.

In a place where people understand him and challenge him and don't hold his age against him, Daniel has become a different child. Learning isn't a fight, so he doesn't fight or act up anymore. Tina no longer has to carry a cell phone everywhere, fearing news of a meltdown. "I don't cry anymore when I drop my son off at school," she says. He has become more confident.

When we talked recently, Daniel had auditioned for a community play and did well enough to be called back. After years of having no real friendships, he now has buddies over every weekend. He still has some assignments and classes that bore him, but because the boredom lasts only a few minutes, not day in and day out, he has learned to cope and entertain himself. He and Tina joke about it, about this "learning to get along" that oils the gears of life. This is possible when he is challenged and learning with his intellectual peers, and it could never have happened if he were kept with children his age.

Daniel is finally learning more about his passion—science. He visited a college chemistry lab recently and met with a professor to ask about taking a class over the summer. The professor tested him with a few math problems, but Daniel could do the algebra necessary for the class in his head, so the professor agreed to let him try. Next year, he'll take some combination of high school and college classes but stay for part of the day with the gifted program at the middle school also. The teacher in that program found Daniel a laminated poster of Einstein for the boy's tenth birthday recently. At least at this middle school Daniel has found they would be okay with another thinker like that.

Daniel deserves an appropriate education as much as any other child. Finally finding it saved this child from misery. Challenging him to the extent of his abilities through this flexible arrangement is costing Tennessee no more than it did when he was in classrooms that didn't meet his needs. If anything, the state is saving money. Nurturing his mind just requires people who believe they can and should do it, who believe providing an appropriate education to a child like Daniel is no more than simple justice.

All highly gifted children need this challenge, flexibility, and understanding. They need teachers and schools that are convinced these children's minds are a national resource that deserves to be developed. They need a culture that values intelligence as the gift it is.

Chance favors the prepared mind, Louis Pasteur once said. Works of genius from grand symphonies to mathematical proofs to speeding up a computer or slowing tumor growth do not just happen. Seeds grow on watered, tended ground.

A nation can choose to deny genius or nurture genius.

We know which world we'd rather live in.

WHETHER YOU HAVE gifted children of your own or just worry about the squandering of America's brightest young minds, you can help create an educational environment that values high achievers and nurtures their gifts. Here are some suggestions for gifted students, parents, educators, mentors, patrons, and policy makers.

WHAT STUDENTS CAN DO

As a gifted student you have more influence in your school and community than you may realize. By thoughtfully communicating your needs and desires for an appropriate education, you can help make your school a better place to learn.

- Realize that being gifted is being different, but there is absolutely nothing wrong with you. Many people do not fit into the one-size-fits-all structure of America's schools. Read about the experiences of other gifted students, the challenges they've faced, and their coping strategies in the Student section of the *Genius Denied* website (www. GeniusDenied.com).
- Don't be afraid to speak up! Many gifted students want to fit in more than anything else, so they may not tell their parents that they constantly are being made to "relearn" what they already know. School exists to help all students learn. Share your frustrations in a polite fashion with your parents and teachers, and talk with them about ways to make your

academic work more challenging. Come to these discussions with practical solutions.

- Teachers may tune out complaints about boredom, but they likely will listen if you show that you already have mastered the material you are being asked to learn. Try suggesting a parallel project you could do instead or a distance-learning option you could substitute.

- Learn how to communicate your concerns calmly and with conviction. Be respectful of others and try to understand their point of view. Sometimes an effective strategy is to show that you understand the other person's position *before* trying to convince him or her of your position.

- Research contests and competitions you would like to participate in. See the GT-CyberSource section of www.Genius Denied.com; search for "competitions" and "gifted programs."

- Read widely and deeply! Find books on subjects that interest you and read as much as you can. Keep a journal. Engage yourself in the community. Join book clubs, attend literary events, join a writers' group, and immerse yourself in language. Get started by looking for book lists online. Check out our list of "Gifted Students' Favorite Books" in the Student section of www.GeniusDenied.com.

- Develop diverse friendships with individuals of different ages. It's okay if many of your friends are older. Friendships are built on shared interests, not on shared birth dates. Ask your parents to help you become involved in mixed-age groups (such as Scout troops or volunteer groups or summer camps) where you can spend time with people of different ages.

- Explore alternative schooling environments. Search the GT-CyberSource on the *Genius Denied* website to find out if your state has schools for gifted students. Search GT-CyberSource for "early college."

- Research policies and laws that affect high-ability learners in your district and state. Write letters, speak at meetings, and help communicate the message that all students, even gifted learners, should have the right to learn in school. You can find information on the gifted policies of your state or the nation in the Policy section of www.GeniusDenied. com.

- Develop your talents. Try to find out what you love to do more than anything else in the world. Ask your parents or family friends or teachers to help you find someone who can teach you the intricacies of your field of interest. You can find tips for forming a learning partnership with a mentor or learning guide in the Student section of www. GeniusDenied.com.

- Use your gifts to help others. Think about what you do well and come up with a plan to share your gifts. To learn about what other gifted young people have done to make a positive difference in the world, go to the Student section of www.GeniusDenied.com.

WHAT PARENTS CAN DO

If you are the parent of a gifted child, realize that your child is exceptional and is likely to have needs that are different from those of other students. Parenting a gifted child can be extra challenging because the child's developmental trajectories vary from the norm. The more gifted the child is, the greater the variance from the norm, and the more the parents will have to adapt their parenting strategies.

- Learn about the characteristics of gifted children. If you suspect your child is gifted, have her assessed. The Library at www.GeniusDenied.com has several articles on identifying gifted children. Search for "characteristics" and "assessment." See also the "Frequently Asked Questions About Giftedness" list in the Parent section.

- Read all you can on giftedness. The needs of gifted young people are often misunderstood. Read what the experts say about various aspects of "being gifted" in the Parent section of www.GeniusDenied.com. To go into greater depth, check out the Library on the *Genius Denied* website for numerous articles on developmental, social-emotional, schooling, talent development and other issues related to being gifted.

- Adopt "gifted-friendly" parenting strategies. Parenting any exceptional child has its challenges; you'll find useful parenting tips in the Parent section of www.GeniusDenied.com.

- Assure your child that it is okay to be different. Highly intelligent children often feel disconnected from their classmates and other age peers. To learn about how gifted children develop friendships, visit the Parent section of www.GeniusDenied.com; look for "Recommended Readings on Friendship."

- Seek out other families with gifted kids, either through area organizations or through your school or community groups. Make sure your child has the opportunity to make friends with children who share her interests.

- Take the time to develop positive relationships with your child's teachers and school administrators. Recognize that they often are doing the best they can given the knowledge they have and the constraints within which they have to work.

- Take your child's complaints of being bored or underchallenged seriously. Teachers and schools are owed respect and a certain amount of leeway, but no child should be subjected to a miserable educational environment.

- Make a point to stay informed about your child's educational experience. Advocate for appropriate placement and a challenging curriculum if your child's educational needs are not being met. See "Parenting Tips on Educational Advocacy" in the Parent section of www.GeniusDenied.com.

- If your child's educational program is not a good match for his or her abilities, develop solutions and ideas before approaching the school. Explore options by brainstorming as a family, conducting research, searching the Internet, and talking with other parents of gifted children. See "Educational Options for Gifted Learners" in the Parent section of www.GeniusDenied.com.

- Hone your advocacy skills. Before asking for a meeting with your child's teacher, learn how to facilitate a successful school meeting. See "Recommended Readings on Educational Advocacy" in the Parent section of www.Genius Denied.com.

- Don't rely on the classroom alone to satisfy your child's desire to learn. Investigate after-school programs, weekend programs, summer classes, and distance-learning experiences. See the GT-CyberSource section.

- Many families with gifted children consider homeschooling because it allows them to individualize the curriculum to match their children's abilities. If you decide to homeschool, the Parent section of www.GeniusDenied.com has some useful tips.

- Consider early college. Highly gifted young people often are ready for the rigor of college-level material before the age of eighteen. One way to explore this option is for your child to take a class at a local community college. Other students explore early college as part of summer talent search programs. You can also search GT-CyberSource at www.Genius Denied.com to see if there are early college experiences or early entrance programs available near you.

- Collaborate with others to start a school for gifted students. Many states have provisions for charter schools for gifted students. Explore the options for new private schools, charter schools, or residential high schools in your state.
- Become active in your local gifted support/advocacy group(s) and/or gifted homeschooling group(s). If one does not exist in your area, start one.
- Highlight learning options in your community that have benefited your child. For example, if your child has a positive experience at the local community college, write a letter to the editor of your local newspaper or contribute the story as a resource for others on the *Genius Denied* website.
- Locate a mentor to support the development of your child's talents and interests. If your child could benefit from working with a mentor, see "Parenting Tips: Finding a Mentor/Learning Guide for Your Gifted Child" in the Parenting Tips submenu of the Parent section at www.GeniusDenied.com.
- Contact local newspapers or TV stations to inform them of academic contests, high-achieving students, or gifted programs, and ask them to do a feature.
- Coach a Math Counts team or get involved in other academic competitions. Search GT-CyberSource to find what competitions are available.
- Learn about the opportunities offered through the regional and national academic talent search programs. See "talent search" in GT-CyberSource.

- Find out if your school district provides professional-development opportunities or in-service training for teachers about the needs of gifted learners. If the district doesn't, ask officials to offer such training.
- Learn about your state's gifted policies. (See the Policy section of www.GeniusDenied.com.)
- Write to your state legislator and ask him or her to sponsor the creation of a residential high school for gifted students.
- Write to your state legislator and ask him or her to sponsor legislation requiring schools to screen students for giftedness and to lower the age of identification to include pre-K and kindergarten. Ask him or her to support legislation mandating that schools meet the educational needs of all who qualify.
- Become involved with the PTA and curriculum selection committees to make sure the needs of gifted students are addressed.
- Join your local or state gifted and talented organization. Become active in bringing about positive change for gifted learners.
- Donate above-grade-level books to an elementary school for in-class libraries.
- Counter stereotypes of gifted students. If parents are talking about acceleration, for instance, and one parent says, "I knew a kid who skipped a few grades and was always miserable," you could bring up a story of a child who made more friends in his new grade and was happier.
- Provide copies of key research articles on gifted issues to teachers and administrators. Full-text articles can be downloaded and printed from the Library section of www. GeniusDenied.com.
- Nominate teachers who challenge gifted students for local

or state teaching awards. Emphasize in the nomination letter that this teacher is helping to solve the widespread problem of underachieving gifted students.

WHAT EDUCATORS CAN DO

High-achieving young people often credit their accomplishments to the help of a caring educator who fueled their interests and guided their learning. Don't miss the opportunity to be this type of educator.

- Learn about the educational needs of gifted learners. See "Recommended Readings for Educators on the Special Needs of Gifted Learners" in the Educator section at www. GeniusDenied.com.
- Take a course on gifted education as part of your certificate renewal or continuing education requirement.
- If you have gifted students in a mixed-ability classroom, learn about curriculum compacting—covering more material in the same amount of time. Design lesson plans using themes rather than specific curricular materials. This will help you adapt the curriculum to each child's ability level while maintaining continuity. Offer more "projects" than worksheets. See "Successful Strategies for Teaching Gifted Learners" in the Educator section of www.GeniusDenied.com.
- Offer students access to books that contain challenging vocabularies and complex themes. Work with your school or community librarians to find challenging books with appropriate content.
- Allow gifted students to work on long-term projects with tangible results. Create opportunities for them to share their

work with their classmates, schoolmates, and the community at large. When appropriate, encourage them to enter their work in competitions.

- Even if your school has a pull-out program, be aware that it may not be a good match for all gifted students. Highly gifted learners need to be grouped with their intellectual peers in more rigorous self-contained academic classes.

- If a student has shown mastery of a concept before the rest of the class, give him permission to work independently on a more challenging project, either in the classroom, in the library, or in the computer lab. Use distance-learning materials. Collaborate with other teachers to see if the child can attend a higher-level class.

- Learn to recognize when a bright child is underachieving in order to "fit in." Offer other opportunities to develop her abilities, such as independent research projects. See "What You Can Do to Reverse Underachievement in Your Classroom" in the Educator section of www.GeniusDenied.com.

- Start discussions with other teachers in the break room or cafeteria about gifted education. Brainstorm what your school and district could do to improve the educational experience for bright children. See "What the Research Says about Gifted Learners" in the Educator section of www.GeniusDenied.com.

- Grade according to each child's ability. For instance, writing "Super" on a gifted writer's essay does little to help nurture her talent. Correct grammatical problems; give her tips on word choice, paragraph order, and persuasiveness. Encourage her family to locate a writing mentor who can develop her talents further.

- Let students from lower grades come to your class for certain subjects if their abilities are a match for your curriculum. Mention this possibility to other teachers in your school.

- Print out articles on gifted education for other educators; see the Library section of www.GeniusDenied.com.
- Share what you learn with your fellow educators to help your school be a place where excellence is encouraged. See "Best Practices of Schools that Nurture Excellence" in the Educator section of www.GeniusDenied.com.
- Help students with particular talents find mentors within the community. For example, introduce a promising young mathematician to a college math professor.
- Lobby your school district to create a magnet school for the gifted or a magnet program within another school.
- Lobby your school to identify gifted children, or if your school already has an identification program, lobby to begin the process in kindergarten.
- If you suspect a child in your class is gifted, send a note home to her parents encouraging them to have her assessed.
- Work collaboratively with parents to better meet the needs of gifted children. Numerous studies confirm that parents provide valuable information about gifted children's abilities and needs and should be consulted in planning educational programs.
- Volunteer to coach academic teams after school. Recruit top students.
- Write or call the university where you received your teaching degree and encourage the school to offer more classes (or a certificate) in gifted education.

What Patrons and Mentors Can Do

Are you interested in changing a life by helping develop a young person's talents? Becoming a patron or mentor will make a significant difference in the life of a talented young person—as well as in your life.

- Learn about the needs of gifted learners. The Library section of www.GeniusDenied.com has numerous articles to inform you about the social, emotional, and intellectual needs of gifted young people.
- Volunteer to become a tutor or mentor in an area in which you have expertise. There are many types of mentoring opportunities. Gifted students often benefit most from "academic" mentoring opportunities. Visit the Mentoring section of www.GeniusDenied.com to learn more.
- Visit the Patrons section of www.GeniusDenied.com for more details on how to become a "Patron of Excellence" in nurturing intellectual development.

What Policy Makers Can Do

Knowledgeable legislators and officials can create thoughtful educational policies that support gifted youth and open the way for them to become high-achieving adults.

- Learn about the educational needs of gifted learners. The Library section of www.GeniusDenied.com has numerous articles to inform you about the social, emotional, and intellectual needs of bright young people.
- Become familiar with your state's or district's educational policies and how they affect high-ability learners. See the Policy section of www.GeniusDenied.com.

- Learn about successful gifted-education policies in other states. See the Policy section of www.GeniusDenied.com.
- Evaluate whether your state or district has policies that interfere with the achievement of high-ability learners. For instance, many states have age requirements on college scholarships or financial aid that keep gifted young people from pursuing higher education when they are ready. Modify or change policies to support high-achieving youth of all ages.
- If your state's laws do not already require schools to identify and serve gifted learners, advocate for or sponsor legislation that will ensure that gifted learners receive an education that nurtures their abilities.

* * *

The *Genius Denied* website, www.GeniusDenied.com, is your resource center for taking action to support our nation's brightest youth. The website features the following:

- More than five hundred articles, including book reviews, op-eds, first person accounts, and biographies, that provide information on the educational, emotional, social, and developmental needs of gifted youth.
- GT-CyberSource, a searchable database of resources for and about gifted and talented young people. Search for information on schools, early college programs, summer programs, contests and competitions, advocacy groups, talent competitions, homeschooling materials, curriculum materials, assessment instruments, and things for fun—books, puzzles, games, software, camps, and places to go.
- Federal policy information and state-by-state gifted education policy information.

- Online forums where site visitors can exchange information and brainstorm strategies for improving gifted education.
- Separate sections with specific information for gifted students, parents, educators, mentors, patrons, and policy-makers.
- News, updates on events, and research in the field of gifted education.
- *Genius Denied* reviews, book excerpts, speech schedules, presentations, book signings, and how to purchase additional copies of *Genius Denied*.

If you have questions or suggestions, or need additional information beyond what is on the *Genius Denied* website, you can contact us at admin@GeniusDenied.com.

Chapter 1: Genius Denied

15 *In the ordinary:* Leta Hollingworth, "What We Know About the Early Selection and Training of Leaders," *Teachers College Record* 40 (1939): 575–92.

15 *Massachusetts, for example, recently:* Bella English, "Brightest Students Lose Out," *Boston Globe*, 20 October 2002, p. 4.

16 *He claimed it was too expensive:* Bill number AB 2626 vetoed 29 September 2002 (online). Legislative Counsel of California, cited 4 April 2003. Available at http://www.leginfo.ca.gov/pub/01-02/bill/asm/ab_2601-2650/ab_2626_vt_20020929.html.

16 *Overall, researcher:* Mary McNamara, "Learn, Baby, Learn," *Los Angeles Times*, 1 April 2001, p. E1.

16 *The number of American students:* Neil J. Dorans, "The Recentering of SAT Scales and Its Effects on Score Distribution and Score Interpretation," Report No. 2002-11. New York: College Board, 2002. Available at http://www.collegeboard.com/repository/200211_20702.pdf. In 1995 the Educational Testing Service recentered the SAT scores and made some modifications in the items on the test. The recentering of the scale had the effect of bringing the scores closer to the midpoint, thus increasing their overall numeric value.

16 *Observers note:* "Part II. The Current Status of Education for the Nation's Most Talented Students," in *National Excellence: A Case for Developing America's Talent* (online). Washington, DC: U.S. Department of Education, 1993, cited 4 April 2003. Available at http://www.ed.gov/pubs/DevTalent/part2.html.

17 *And HERI's 2002:* Shaena Engle, "College Freshmen Spend Less Time Studying and More Time Surfing the Net, UCLA Survey Reveals" (online). Higher Education Research Institute, UCLA Graduate School of Education and Information Studies, 2003, cited 4 April 2003. Available at http://www.gseis.ucla.edu/heri/02_press_release.pdf.

19 *The U.S. Department:* U.S. Department of Education, Office of Educational Research and Improvement, *National Excellence: A Case for Developing America's Talent* (Washington, DC: U.S. Government Printing Office, 1993).

22 *As Dr. Julian Stanley:* Camilla P. Benbow and Julian C. Stanley, "Inequity in Equity: How 'Equity' Can Lead to Inequity in High Potential Students," *Psychology, Public Policy, and Law* 2 (1996): 279.

CHAPTER 2: THE SORRY STATE OF GIFTED EDUCATION

29 *For the Missouri Department:* "About the Gifted Education Program" (online). Jefferson City, Missouri: Missouri Department of Elementary and Secondary Education, 2003, cited 4 April 2003. Available at http://www.dese.state.mo.us/divimprove/gifted/abgifted.html.

33 *And so, in a good district:* Multiple calls to the gifted coordinator for Paul's school were not returned.

34 *Only twenty-nine states:* Council of State Directors of Programs of the Gifted, *State of the States Gifted and Talented Education Report 2001–2002* (Longmont, CO: Council of State Directors of Programs for the Gifted and National Association for Gifted Children, 2003) p. 48, 58.

34 *One classroom study:* "Part II. The Current Status of Education for the Nation's Most Talented Students," in *National Excellence: A Case for Developing America's Talent* (online). Washington, DC: U.S. Department of Education, 1993, cited 4 April 2003. Available at http://www.ed.gov/pubs/DevTalent/part2.html.

34 *Teachers most often individualized:* ibid.

34 *According to the 1993:* ibid.

36 *State budgets for gifted:* Council of the State Directors of Programs of the Gifted, *State of the States Gifted and Talented Education Report 2001–2002* (Longmont, CO: Council of State Directors of Programs for Gifted and National Association for Gifted Children, 2003), pp. 150–52.

36 *The fifty states:* Jay G. Chambers, Thomas B. Parrish, and Jenifer J. Harr, *What Are We Spending on Special Education Services in the United States, 1999–2000?* Report number 02-01, Special Education Expenditure Project, March 2, 2002 (Washington, DC: Center

for Special Education Finance, Office of Special Education Program, U.S. Department of Education, 2002).

37 *This landmark special:* Education for All Handicapped Children Act of 1975, Public Law 94-142 (S. 6), 29 November 1975. Available at http://www.asclepius.com/angel/special.html.

38 *The numbers are staggering:* "President Bush Asks Congress for $1.8 Billion for Pennsylvania's Students" (online). Washington, DC: U.S. Department of Education, 4 February 2002, cited 4 April 2003. Available at http://www.ed.gov/news/pressreleases/2002/02/state-by-state/pennsylvania.html.

"President Bush Asks Congress for $1.6 Billion for Michigan's Students" (online). Washington, DC: U.S. Department of Education, 4 February 2002, cited 4 April 2003. Available at http://www.ed.gov/news/pressreleases/2002/02/state-by-state/michigan.html.

"President Bush Asks Congress for $5.8 Billion for California's Students" (online). Washington, DC: U.S. Department of Education, 4 February 2002, cited 4 April 2003. Available at http://www.ed.gov/news/pressreleases/2002/02/state-by-state/california.html.

39 *And 84 percent:* "Part II. The Current Status of Education for the Nation's Most Talented Students."

40 *"Given the State's":* Assembly Bill number 2626 vetoed 09/29/2002. Legislative Counsel of California, cited 4 April 2003. Available at http://www.leginfo.ca.gov/pub/01-02/bill/asm/ab_2601 2650/ab_2626_vt_20020929.html. Governor Davis's veto letter stated, "This bill creates additional General Fund pressures of more than $1 million a year. Moreover it requires the State for the first time to pay more than is required by current law to educate a student at the California Community Colleges. Given the State's current fiscal situation, I cannot sign this measure."

41 *No wonder California:* Valory Mitchell, "La Suer Says Education Governor's Veto of AB 2626 Is a Slap in the Face to 'California's Highly Gifted Students'" (online). California assemblyman Jay La Suer's website, 1 October 2002, cited 4 April 2003. Available at http://republican.assembly.ca.gov/members/index.asp?Dist=77& Lang=1&Body=PressReleases&RefID=559.

49 *Many researchers consider:* "Why Should Gifted Education Be Sup-

ported?" (online). Washington, DC: National Association of Gifted Students, cited 4 April 2003. Available at http://www.nagc.org/ParentInfo.

CHAPTER 3: THE LOWEST COMMON DENOMINATOR

51 *"There is in America":* Margaret Mead, "The Gifted Child in the American Culture of Today," *Journal of Teacher Education* 5 (1954): 211–14.

52 *In the 1830s:* Alexis de Tocqueville, "Why the Americans Are More Addicted to Practical Than to Theoretical Science," in *Democracy in America,* trans. Henry Reeve (New York: Longmans, Green, 1889).

52 *Children have always:* Richard Hofstadter, *Anti-Intellectualism in American Life* (New York: Vintage, 1962), p. 307.

53 *Take away his philosophy:* Sarah Mondale and Sarah B. Patton, eds., *School: The Story of American Public Education* (Boston: Beacon Press, 2002), p. 25.

53 *Enrollment in public schools:* ibid, p. 58.

54 *"Provision should be made":* Hofstadter, p. 336.

54 *Then, in the 1950s:* ibid., p. 345, and chapter 13, "The Road to Life Adjustment."

54 *Hofstadter cites:* ibid., pp. 354–55. Hofstadter cites Griswold, A. Whitney, *Liberal Education and the Democratic Ideal* (New Haven, CT: Yale University Press, 1959), p. 29; the case was first reported by Griswold in 1954.

59 *"The sorting of students":* Anne Wheelock, *Crossing the Tracks: How "Untracking" Can Save America's Schools* (New York: The New Press, 1992), p. 6.

60 *In 1997, ACORN:* "Secret Apartheid II" (online). New York: ACORN Schools Office, 1997, cited 2 April 2003. Available at http://www.acorn.org/ACORNarchives/studies/secretapartheid2.

60 *It also claimed:* ibid.

61 *Yet rather than demanding:* "Secret Apartheid I" (online). New York: ACORN Schools Office, cited 2 April 2003. Available at http://www.acorn.org/ACORNarchives/studies/secretapartheid.

62 *One education writer:* Jeannie Oakes, *Keeping Track: How Schools Structure Inequality* (New Haven, CT: Yale University Press, 1985), p. 210.

65   *The most recent:* Council of State Directors of Programs of the Gifted, *State of the States Gifted and Talented Education Report 2001–2002* (Longmont, CO: Council of State Directors of Programs for the Gifted and National Association for Gifted Children, 2003), p. 136, 148.

66   *A 2003 survey:* Francis A. Karnes, Kristen R. Stephens, and James E. Whorton, "Certification and Specialized Competencies for Teachers in Gifted Education Programs," *Roeper Review* 22 (2003): 201–2.

66   *A Gifted Child Quarterly study:* J. B. Hansen and J. F. Feldhusen, "Comparison of Trained and Untrained Teachers of Gifted Students," *Gifted Child Quarterly* 38, no. 3 (1994): 115–21.

67   *NBPTS offers:* National Board for Professional Teaching Standards, Candidate Resource Center, 2002 (online), cited 2 April 2003. Available at http://www.nbpts.org/candidates/ckc.cfm.

67   *Unfortunately,* "Giftedness Education": "The Death of Giftedness" in James Borland, ed., *Rethinking Gifted Education* (New York: Teachers College Press, 2003).

70   *But rather than urge:* Oakes, p. 194.

70   *"Segregation of students":* National Council for Teachers of English, "Tracked for Failure/Tracked for Success" (online), cited 2 April 2003. Available at http://www.ncte.org/about/over/positions/level/elem/107685.htm.

71   *When James Kulik:* James A. Kulik, "An Analysis of the Research on Ability Grouping: Historical and Contemporary Perspectives," Research-Based Decision Making Series (Storrs: National Research Center on the Gifted and Talented, University of Connecticut, 1992), pp. vii–viii. Available from ERIC, ED 350777.

71   *Studies of this grouping:* ibid.

71   *As for the issue:* Oakes, pp. 143–44.

71   *Researchers have found:* Kulik.

72   *Critics claim that:* Oakes.

73   *Programs for the gifted mean:* Mara Sapon-Shevin, *Playing Favorites: Gifted Education and the Disruption of Community* (Albany: State University of New York Press, 1994), pp. 181–234.

73   *We do know:* "Mainstream Science on Intelligence," *The Wall Street Journal,* 13 December 1994, cited in L. S. Gottfredson, "Mainstream Science on Intelligence: An Editorial with 52 Signatories, History and Bibliography." *Intelligence* 24 (1997): 13–23.

75   *Jonathan Kozol:* Jonathan Kozol, *Savage Inequalities: Children in America's Schools.* (New York: HarperCollins, 1992), p. 108.

76   *Then we will have:* ibid, p. 186.

CHAPTER 4: PARENTING PUSHY KIDS

81   *Research shows that parents:* Benjamin S. Bloom, ed., *Developing Talent in Young People* (New York: Ballantine, 1985).
     Ellen Winner, *Gifted Children: Myths and Realities* (New York: Basic Books, 1996).

82   *They've never been challenged:* Patricia A. Schuler, "Perfectionism and Gifted Adolescents," *Journal of Secondary Gifted Education* 16, no. 4 (2000): 183–96.

82   *According to the National:* "Why Should Gifted Education Be Supported?" (online). Washington, DC: National Association of Gifted Students, cited 4 April 2003. Available at http://www.nagc.org/ParentInfo.

83   *Studies also indicate:* Maureen Neihart and F. Richard Olenchak, *The Social and Emotional Development of Gifted Children: What Do We Know?* (Waco, TX: Prufrock Press, 2002), p. 168.

84   *Clay Shrout:* "Secret Service Studies Shootings," 15 August 2000 (online). CBS News, *60 Minutes II*, cited 7 April 2003. Available at http://www.cbsnews.com.

84   *Even though he has:* "Dr. William Sack's Evaluation of Kinkel" (online). PBS Online and WGBH/*Frontline*, 2000, cited 7 April 2003. Available at http://www.pbs.org/wgbh/pages/frontline/shows/kinkel/trial/sack.html.

85   *Some gifted minority:* Sylvia Rimm, "Social Adjustment and Peer Pressures for Gifted Children" (online). Davidson Institute for Talent Development, 2003, cited 7 April 2003. Available at http://www.gt-cybersource.org.

85   *Gifted teenage girls:* Joan Franklin Smutny, "Gifted Girls," *Understanding Our Gifted* 11, no. 2 (1999): 9–13.

89   *Recently, puzzle designer:* Scott Kim, "Bogglers," *Discover* 24, no. 6 (June 2003): 80.

90   *According to Gina:* Gina Ginsburg, *How to Help Your Gifted Child: A Handbook for Parents and Teachers* (New York: Monarch Press, 1977).

95   *The most highly gifted:* Miraca Gross, "The Pursuit of Excellence or the Search for Intimacy? The Forced Choice Dilemma of Gifted Youth," *Roeper Review* (1989): 189–94. Gross describes "a dilemma peculiar to gifted youth" that "arises through the interaction of the psychosocial drives towards intimacy and achievement, which complement each other in students of average ability, but which place the gifted student in a forced-choice situation. If the gifted child chooses to satisfy the drive for excellence, he or she must risk forfeiting the attainment of intimacy with age peers; if the choice is intimacy, the gifted may be forced into a pattern of systematic and deliberate underachievement to retain membership in the social group." Homogeneous grouping of gifted students is suggested as a partial solution to this dilemma.

CHAPTER 5: PATRONS, TEACHERS, AND MENTORS

104   *Research shows that childhood:* Benjamin S. Bloom, ed., *Developing Talent in Young People* (New York: Ballantine, 1985).

105   *Society needs world-class:* A quote from Lauren A. Sosniak and Judith A. Monsaas in Bloom, ed., *Developing Talent in Young People.* Bloom's research concluded that concerns about time pressure on talented children who need time to play and "just be kids" are exaggerated, noting that the highly accomplished subjects of his study spent about the same amount of time on their disciplined practice as did their age peers on TV viewing.

107   *"Some people may":* Laura Vanderkam, "SAT Talent Searches Lead Nowhere for Many," *USA Today,* 20 January 2003, p. 13A.

108   *A study of these:* James R. Campbell, A. Feng, and M. Verna, "1999 United States Olympiad Studies: Math, Physics, Chemistry." Paper presented at the Thirteenth Biennial World Conference of the World Council for Gifted and Talented Children. Cited in James Reed Campbell, Harold Wagner, and Herbert J. Walberg, "Academic Competitions and Programs Designed to Challenge the Exceptionally Talented," in *International Handbook of Giftedness and Talent,* 2d ed., rev., edited by Kurt A. Heller et al., (Amsterdam: Elsevier Science, 2000), pp. 529–34.

109   *These relationships:* ibid.

109   *Liz Baker:* Vanderkam, p. 13A.

110 *"Without you, without":* Herbert R. Lottman, *Albert Camus: A Biography.* (Garden City, NY: Doubleday, 1979), p. 609.

111 *She developed many:* Barbara Lourie Sand, *Teaching Genius: Dorothy DeLay and the Making of a Musician* (Portland, OR: Amadeus Press, 2000), pp. 67–71.

117 *The International Telementoring Program: History* (online). International Telementor Program, cited 1 April 2003. Available at http://www.telementor.org/aboutus.cfm.

118 *Tahlequah High School:* Betty Smith, "Gifted, Talented Students Follow Mentors' Lead," *Oklahoma Tahlequah Daily Press,* 10 February 2003.

CHAPTER 6: SCHOOL SOLUTIONS: "I DO NOT SEE BOREDOM HERE"

138 *Since former North Carolina:* Penny Britton Kolloff, "State-Supported Residential High Schools," in *Handbook of Gifted Education,* 3rd ed., edited by Nicholas Colangelo and Gary A. Davis (New York: Pearson Education, 2003), pp. 238–46.

141 *For some . . . acceleration:* James Borland, "Foreword." In *The Academic Acceleration of Gifted Children,* edited by S. Thomas Southern, Eric D. Jones, and William T. Southern (New York: Teachers College Press, 1991): vii–viii. Cited in Miraca Gross, "Radical Acceleration: Responding to Academic and Social Needs of Extremely Gifted Adolescents," *Journal of Secondary Gifted Education* 5, no. 4 (1994).

141 *As one gifted girl:* Carol, a highly gifted eighth grade girl, cited in Gross, "Radical Acceleration."

142 *These studies showed:* James A. Kulik and Chen-Lin C. Kulik, "Synthesis of Research on Effects of Accelerated Instruction," *Educational Leadership* 42 (1984): 84–89. After reviewing the results of twenty-six studies, the authors concluded that "talented youngsters who were accelerated into higher grades performed as well as the talented older pupils already in those grades. In the subjects in which they were accelerated, talented accelerates showed almost a year's advancement over talented same-age nonaccelerates."

143 *They enjoyed closer:* Miraca Gross, "The Use of Radical Acceleration in Cases of Extreme Intellectual Precocity," *Gifted Child Quarterly*

36, no. 2 (1992): 91–99. Miraca Gross, *Exceptionally Gifted Children* (New York: Routledge, 1993).

143   *Long-term studies:* Paul M. Janos et al., "A Cross-Sectional Developmental Study of the Social Relations of Students Who Enter College Early," *Gifted Child Quarterly* 32 (1988): 210–15.

143   *Although the research:* Based upon our experience at the Davidson Institute for Talent Development serving approximately four hundred Davidson Young Scholars from 1999 through 2003.

144   *The Iowa Acceleration:* Colleen Harsin, "Iowa Acceleration Scale—A Tool for Evaluating Appropriate Placement for Gifted Learners" (online). Available at http://www.gt-cybersource.org.

145   *What promotion:* David Elkind, "Acceleration," *Young Children* 43, no. 4 (May 1988): 2.

147   *"I went because":* Laura Vanderkam, "Some Can Sail Over High School," *USA Today*, 6 August 2002. Available at http://www.gt-cybersource.org.

152   *States have a variety:* Brian D. Ray, House Education Committee of the Commonwealth of Pennsylvania, *House Education Committee Hearing for HB 2560* (online). Harrisburg, Pennsylvania, 13 June 2002, cited 8 April 2003. Available at http://members.truevine.net/pilgrimspage@truevine.net/BRaytestimony020613.htm.

Chapter 7: Raising the Ceiling and the Floor

157   *"No one explains":* Judy Galbraith, "The Eight Great Gripes of Gifted Kids: Responding to Special Needs," *Roeper Review* 8 (1985): 15–18. Follow-up study: Mark A. Kunkel et al., "Experiences of Giftedness: 'Eight Great Gripes' Six Years Later," *Roeper Review* 15, no. 19 (1992): 10–14. The other great gripes were (2) "The stuff we do in school is too easy and it's boring"; (3) "Parents, teachers, and friends expect us to be perfect, to 'do our best' all the time"; (4) "Kids often tease us about being smart"; (5) "Friends who really understand us are far and few between"; (6) "We feel too different and wish people would accept us for what we are"; (7) "We feel overwhelmed by the number of things we can do in life"; (8) "We worry a lot about world problems and feel helpless to do anything about them."

159   *"The problem is not":* Daniel J. Singal, "The Other Crisis in American Education," *Atlantic Monthly* 268, no. 5 (1991): 59–74.

166   *The state of Idaho:* Idaho's Gifted and Talented Mandate and Mission Statement, cited 17 July 2003, at http://www.sde.state.id.us/GiftedTalented/mandate.

166   The Boise schools: Boise Schools' Gifted and Talented Program, cited 23 July 2003, at http://www.boiseschools.org/esc/staff/gate.html.

"About the Gifted Education Program" (online). Jefferson City, Missouri: Missouri Department of Elementary and Secondary Education, 2003 (cited 4 April 2003). Available at http://www.dese.state.mo.us/divimprove/gifted/abgifted.html.

Aizenman, Nurith C. "Students Complicated Gifts: Schools Struggle with Exceptional Learning Disabled." *Washington Post,* 23 June 2002, sec. A, p. 1.

Albert, Robert S. "The Contribution of Early Family History to the Achievement of Eminence." In *Talent Development,* vol. 2, ed. by Nicholas Colangelo and Susan Assouline (Dayton, OH: Ohio Psychology Press, 1994).

———. "Exceptionally Gifted Boys and Their Parents." *Gifted Child Quarterly* 24, no. 4 (1980): 174–79.

———. *Genius and Eminence.* Edited by Michael Argyle, 6 vols. Vol. 5, *International Series in Experimental Social Psychology* (Elmsford, NY: Pergamon Press, 1983).

Allan, Susan D. "Ability-Grouping Research Reviews: What Do They Say About Grouping and the Gifted?" *Educational Leadership* (1991): 60–67.

Archambault, Francis X. Jr., et al. "Regular Classroom Practices with Gifted Students: Result of a National Survey of Classroom Teachers" (Storrs: National Research Center on the Gifted and Talented, University of Connecticut, 1993).

Assouline, Susan. "Psychological and Educational Assessment of Gifted Children." In *Handbook of Gifted Education,* ed. by Nicholas Colangelo and Gary Davis (Boston: Allyn and Bacon, 2003), pp. 124–45.

Assouline, Susan, and Nicholas Colangelo. "Self-Concept of Gifted Students." *TEMPO, Texas Association for Gifted Newsletter* 15, no. 3 (1995): 5–8.

Assouline, Susan, and Ann E. Lupkowski. "Extending the Talent Search Model: The Potential of the SSAT-Q for Identification of Mathematically Talented Elementary Students." In *Proceedings of the Henry B. and*

Jocelyn Wallace National Research Symposium on Talent Development, ed. by Nicholas Colangelo, Susan Assouline, and DeAnn Ambroson (New York: Trillium Press, 1992), pp. 223–32.

Assouline, Susan, and Ann E. Lupkowski-Shoplik. "Talent Searches: A Model for the Discovery and Development of Academic Talent." In *Handbook of Gifted Education*, ed. by Nicholas Colangelo and Gary Davis (Boston: Allyn & Bacon, 1997), pp. 170–79.

Assouline, Susan, and Ann Shoplik. *Developing Mathematical Talent: A Guide for Teachers and Parents of Gifted Students* (Waco, TX: Prufrock Press, 2002).

Baker, Jean A., Robert Bridger, and Karen Evans. "Models of Underachievement Among Gifted Preadolescents: The Role of Personal, Family, and School Factors." *Gifted Child Quarterly* 42, no. 1 (1998): 5–15.

Baldwin, Alexinia Y. "Programs for the Gifted and Talented: Issues Concerning Minority Populations." In *The Gifted and Talented: Developmental Perspectives*, ed. by Francis Degen Horowitz and Marion O'Brian (Washington, DC: American Psychological Association, 1985), pp. 197–221.

Banks, David. "Clusters of Talent" (online). *Classification Society of North America Newsletter* 48 (1997) (cited 10 April 2003). Available at http://www.pitt.edu/~csna/news/csna.news48.html.

Benbow, Camilla Persson, and David Lubinski, eds. *Intellectual Talent* (Baltimore, MD: Johns Hopkins University Press, 1996).

Benbow, Camilla Persson, David Lubinski, and Hossain E. Sanjani. "Our Future Leaders in Science: Who Are They? Can We Identify Them Early?" In *Talent Development*, vol. 3, ed. by Nicholas Colangelo and Susan Assouline (Scottsdale, AZ: Gifted Psychology Press, 1999), pp. 59–70.

Benbow, Camilla Persson, and Lola L. Minor. "Cognitive Profiles of Verbally and Mathematically Precocious Students." *Gifted Child Quarterly* 34, no. 1 (1990): 21–26.

Benbow, Camilla Persson, and Julian C. Stanley. "An Eight-Year Evaluation of SMPY: What Was Learned?" In *Academic Precocity: Aspects of Its Development*, ed. by C. P. Benbow and J. C. Stanley (Baltimore, MD: Johns Hopkins University Press, 1983), pp. 205–14.

———. "Inequity in Equity: How Equity Can Lead to Inequity in High Potential Students." In *Psychology, Public Policy, and Law* (Washington, DC: American Psychological Association, 1996), pp. 249–92.

Benson, Etienne. "Intelligent Intelligence Testing: Psychologists Are Broadening the Concept of Intelligence and How to Test It." *Monitor on Psychology* (2003): 48–51.

Berger, Sandra. *College Planning for Gifted Students,* 2d ed. rev. (Reston, VA: Council for Exceptional Children, 1998).

———. "Mentor Relationships and Gifted Learners." ERIC Digest #E486, 1990.

———. "Supporting Gifted Education Through Advocacy." ERIC (Educational Resources Information Center) Digest #E494, 1990.

Bernstein, Harriet T. "New Politics of Textbook Adoption." *Phi Delta Kappan* (March 1985): 463–66.

Betts, George, and Maureen Neihart. "Profiles of the Gifted and Talented." *Gifted Child Quarterly* 32, no. 2 (1988).

Blair, Julie. "Study Says School Atmosphere Fosters Abuse of 'Nerds.'" *Education Week* 22, no. 23 (2003): 10.

Bloom, Benjamin S., ed. *Developing Talent in Young People* (New York: Ballantine, 1985).

———. "The Role of Gifts and Markers in the Development of Talent." *Exceptional Children* 48, no. 6 (1982): 510–21.

Bloom, Benjamin, and Lauren Sosniak. "Talent Development vs. Schooling." *Educational Leadership* 32, no. 2 (1981): 86–94.

Bloom, Harold. *Genius: A Mosaic of One Hundred Exemplary Creative Minds* (New York: Warner Books, 2002).

Borland, James. "Foreword." In *The Academic Acceleration of Gifted Children,* ed. by S. Thomas Southern, Eric D. Jones, and William T. Southern (New York: Teachers College Press, 1991).

———. "IQ Tests: Throwing Out the Bath Water, Saving the Baby." *Roeper Review* 8, no. 3 (1986): 163–67.

———. "The Death of Giftedness: Gifted Education Without Gifted Children." In *Rethinking Gifted Education,* ed. by James H. Borland (New York: Teachers College Press, 2003).

Braddock, Jomills Henry II, and Robert E. Slavin. "Why Ability Grouping Must End: Achieving Excellence and Equity in American Education." Paper presented at the Common Destiny Conference, Johns Hopkins University, Baltimore, MD, September 1992.

Breslin, Meg McSherry. "More Thought to Gifted Pupils: River Forest Schools Aim to Keep Brightest from Being Left Behind." *Chicago Tribune,* 1 December 2002, p. 1.

Brice, Jessica. *Committee Passes Bill to Let Gifted Students Skip High School* (online). SignOnSanDiego.com, 2002 (cited 20 August 2002). Available at http://www.signonsandiego.com.

Brody, Linda E. "The Talent Searches: Counseling and Mentoring Activities." In *Talent Development*, vol. 3, ed. by Nicholas Colangelo and Susan Assouline (Baltimore, MD: Johns Hopkins University Press, 1983), pp. 205–12.

Brody, Linda, Susan Assouline, and Julian Stanley. "Five Years of Early Entrants: Predicting Successful Achievement in College." *Gifted Child Quarterly* 34, no. 4 (1990): 138–42.

Brody, Linda, and Carol Blackburn. "Nurturing Exceptional Talent: SET as a Legacy of SMPY." In *Intellectual Talent: Psychometric and Social Issues*, ed. by Camilla Persson Benbow and David Lubinski (Baltimore, MD: Johns Hopkins University Press, 1996), pp. 246–65.

Brody, Linda E., and Carol J. Miles. "Gifted Children with Learning Disabilities: A Review of the Issues." *Journal of Learning Disabilities* 30, no. 3 (1997): 282–86.

Bull, Barry L. "Eminence and Precocity: An Examination of the Justification of Education for the Gifted and Talented." *Teachers College Record* 87, no. 1 (1985): 1–19.

Bynog, David. *A Brief History of Patronage* (online). Rice University, 2001 (cited 25 June 2002). Available at http://es.rice.edu/ES/humsoc/Galileo/Student_Work/Florence96/jessdave/patronage.html.

Callahan, Carolyn M., and Evelyn Levsky Hiatt. "Assessing and Nurturing Talent in a Diverse Culture: What Do We Do, What Should We Do, What Can We Do?" In *Talent in Context: Historical and Social Perspectives on Giftedness*, ed. by Reva C. Friedman and Karen B. Rogers (Washington, DC: American Psychological Association, 1998), pp. 3–15.

Campanile, Carl. "Girl Sues NY to be Grad at 14." *New York Post*, 21 April 2003.

Campbell, James R. "Secrets of Award-Winning Programs for Gifted in Mathematics." *Gifted Child Quarterly* 32, no. 4 (1988): 326–65.

Campbell, James R., A. Feng, and M. Verna. "1999 United States Olympiad Studies: Math, Physics, Chemistry." Paper presented at the Thirteenth Biennial World Conference of the World Council for Gifted and Talented Children. See also James Reed Campbell, Harold Wagner, and Herbert J. Walberg, "Academic Competitions and Programs

Designed to Challenge the Exceptionally Talented," in *International Handbook of Giftedness and Talent*, 2d ed. rev., ed. by Kurt A. Heller et al. (Amsterdam: Elsevier Science, 2000), pp. 529–34.

Campbell, James R., Harald Wagner, and Herbert J. Walberg. "Academic Competitions and Programs Designed to Challenge the Exceptionally Talented." In *International Handbook of Giftedness and Talent*, ed. by Kurt A. Heller et al. (Amsterdam: Elsevier Science, 2000), pp. 523–35.

Capurro, Marie L. "Pursuing Profound Possibilities: The Davidson Institute for Talent Development" (online). Reno, NV: Davidson Institute for Talent Development, 2001 (cited 9 April 2003). Available at http://www.gt-cybersource.org.

———. "Teacher to Teacher: Teaching Highly Gifted Students in the Regular Classroom" (online). Reno, NV: Davidson Institute for Talent Development, 2003 (cited 9 April 2003). Available at http://www.ditd.org/cybersource/record.aspx?sid=11201&scat=902&stype=110.

Carlton, Sandra. "Parent-Educator Relationships." *Understanding Our Gifted* (Nov. 1990): 13.

Carroll, John B. "Psychometrics, Intelligence, and Public Perception." *Intelligence* 24, no. 1 (1997): 25–52.

Cashion, Marie, and Karon Sullenger. " 'Contact Us Next Year': Tracing Teachers' Use of Gifted Practices." *Roeper Review* 23, no. 1 (2000): 18–21.

Cerovsek, Corey. "First Person Perspective on the Early College Experience" (online). Reno, NV: The Davidson Institute for Talent Development, 2003 (cited 9 April 2003). Available at http://www.gt-cybersource.org.

Chambers, Jay, Thomas B. Parrish, and Jenifer J. Harr. "What Are We Spending on Special Education Services in the United States, 1999–2000?" (Washington, DC: United States Department of Education, Office of Special Education Programs, 2002).

Charlton, Jane C., et al. "Follow-Up Insights on Rapid Acceleration." *Roeper Review* 17, no. 2 (1994): 123–30.

Clark, Barbara. "Social Ideologies and Gifted Education in Today's Schools." *Peabody Journal of Education* 72, no. 3–4 (1997): 81–99.

———. *Growing Up Gifted: Developing the Potential of Children at Home and at School*, 6th ed. (Saddle River, NJ: Prentice Hall, 2001).

Cognard, Anne M. *The Case for Weighting Grades and Waiving Classes for Gifted and Talented High School Students* (RM96226). (Storrs: National

Research Center on the Gifted and Talented, University of Connecticut, 1966).

Colangelo, Nicholas. "Academically Talented Students: They Don't Think the Way We Think They Think." In *Talent Development: Proceedings from the 1998 Henry B. and Jocelyn Wallace National Research Symposium on Talent Development,* ed. by Nicholas Colangelo and Susan Assouline (Scottsdale, AZ: Great Potential Press, 2001), pp. 3–9.

———. "Counseling Gifted Students." In *Handbook of Gifted Education,* ed. by Nicholas Colangelo and Gary A. Davis (Boston: Allyn and Bacon, 1991, 1997, 2003).

———. "Moral Dilemmas as Formulated by Gifted Students." *Understanding Our Gifted* 1, no. 1 (1989): 10–12.

———. "Psychological Development of Gifted Students." *Exceptionality Education Canada* 1, no. 1 (1991): 103–17.

Colangelo, Nicholas, and Susan Assouline. "Counseling Gifted Students." In *International Handbook of Giftedness and Talent,* ed. by Kurt A. Heller et al. (Amsterdam: Elsevier Science, 2000).

———. "Self-Concept of Gifted Students: Patterns by Self-Concept Domain, Grade Level, and Gender." In *Nurturing Talent: Individual Needs and Social Ability,* ed. by Michael W. Katzko and Franz J. Monks (Assen, The Netherlands: Van Gorcum, 1995), pp. 66–74.

Colangelo, Nicholas, and Gary Davis. "Introduction." In *Handbook of Gifted Education,* ed. by Nicholas Colangelo and Gary Davis (Boston: Allyn and Bacon, 2003), pp. 3–10.

Colangelo, Nicholas, and David F. Dettmann. "A Review of Research on Parents and Families of Gifted Children." *Exceptional Children* 50, no. 1 (1983): 20–27.

Colangelo, Nicholas, and Barbara Kerr. "Extreme Academic Talent Profiles of Perfect Scorers." *Journal of Educational Psychology* 82, no. 3 (1990): 404–9.

Colangelo, Nicholas, et al. "Parental Involvement in the Academic and Social Lives of Academically Talented Elementary School Students." In *Talent Development: Proceedings from the 1995 Henry B. and Jocelyn Wallace National Research Symposium on Talent Development,* ed. by Nicholas Colangelo and Susan Assouline (Scottsdale, AZ: Gifted Psychology Press, 1999), pp. 307–13.

Colangelo, Nicholas, et al. "A Comparison of Gifted Underachievers and Gifted High Achievers." *Gifted Child Quarterly* 37 (1993): 155–60.

Colangelo, Nicholas, et al. *Young Inventors.* (Iowa City: Connie Belin and Jacqueline N. Blank International Center for Gifted Education and Talent Development, University of Iowa, 2002), 1–21.

Colangelo, Nicholas, et al. "The Iowa Inventiveness Inventory: Toward a Measure of Mechanical Inventiveness." *Creativity Research Journal* 5, no. 2 (1992): 157–63.

Coleman, Laurence J., and Tracy L. Cross. *Being Gifted in School: An Introduction to Development, Guidance and Teaching.* (Waco, TX: Prufrock Press, 2001).

———. "Social-Emotional Development and Personal Experience of Giftedness." In *International Handbook of Giftedness and Talent,* ed. by Kurt A. Heller et al. (Amsterdam: Elsevier Science, 2000), pp. 203–12.

Collin, W. Andrew, et al. "Contemporary Research on Parenting: The Case for Nature and Nurture." *American Psychologist* 55 (2000): 218–32.

Council of State Directors of Programs of the Gifted. *State of the States Gifted and Talented Education Report 2001–2002* (Longmont, CO: Council of State Directors of Programs for the Gifted and National Association for Gifted Children, 2003), pp. 48, 58, 136, 148, and 150–52.

Cronbach, Lee J. "Acceleration Among the Terman Males: Correlates in Midlife and After." In *Intellectual Talent,* ed. by Camilla Persson Benbow and David Lubinski (Baltimore, MD: Johns Hopkins University Press, 1996), 179–91.

Cronin, Anne. "Asynchronous Parenting" (online). Reno, NV: Davidson Institute for Talent Development, 2002 (cited 9 April 2003). Available at http://www.ditd.org/cybersource/record.aspx?sid=11506&scat=902&stype=110.

Cross, Tracy L. *On the Social and Emotional Lives of Gifted Children* (Waco, TX: Prufrock Press, 2000).

———. "Psychological and Social Aspects of Educating Gifted Students." *Peabody Journal of Education* 72, no. 4 (1997).

Cross, Tracy L., Karyn Gust-Brey, and P. Bonny Ball. "A Psychological Autopsy of the Suicide of an Academically Gifted Student: Researchers' and Parents' Perspectives." *Gifted Child Quarterly* 46, no. 4 (2002).

Csikszentmihalyi, Mihaly. *Beyond Boredom and Anxiety: Experiencing Flow in Work and Play.* San Francisco: Jossey-Bass, 2000.

———. "Creativity Across the Life-Span: A Systems View." In *Talent Development,* vol. 3, ed. by Nicholas Colangelo and Susan Assouline (Baltimore, MD: Johns Hopkins University Press, 1983).

————. *Finding Flow: The Psychology of Engagement with Everyday Life* (New York: Basic Books, 1997).

————. *Talented Teenagers: The Roots of Success and Failure* (Cambridge, Eng.: Cambridge University Press, 2000).

Csikszentmihalyi, Mihaly, Kevin Rathunde, and Samuel Whalen. *Talented Teenagers* (New York: Cambridge University Press, 1993).

Cullum, Lee. *Genius Came Early: Creativity in the Twentieth Century*, 2d ed. (Austin, TX: Windsor House, 1999).

Cutrona, Carolyn E., et al. "Parental Society Support and Academic Achievement: An Attachment Theory Perspective." *Journal of Personality and Social Psychology* 66, no. 2 (1994): 369–78.

Daggett Pollins, Lynn. "The Effects of Acceleration on the Social and Emotional Development of Gifted Students." In *Academic Precocity: Affects of Its Development*, ed. by Camilla Persson Benbow and Julian C. Stanley (Baltimore, MD: Johns Hopkins University Press, 1983), pp. 160–78.

Dauber, Susan, and Camilla Persson Benbow. "Aspects of Personality and Peer Relations of Extremely Talented Adolescents." *Gifted Child Quarterly* 34, no. 1 (1990): 10–14.

Davies, Peter J. *The Character of a Genius: Beethoven in Perspective* (Westport, CT: Greenwood Press, 2002).

Deakin, Michelle Bates. "Course Correction" (online). *Boston Globe Magazine*, 8 June 2003 (cited 1 August, 2003). Available at http://www.boston.com/globe/magazine/2003/0608/coverstory.htm.

Delcurt, Marcia A. B. "Creative Productivity Among Secondary School Students: Combining Energy, Interest, and Imagination." *Gifted Child Quarterly* 37 (1993): 3–31.

Delisle, James R. *Gifted Children Speak Out* (Minneapolis, MN: Free Spirit Publishing, 1987).

————. "In Praise of Elitism." *Gifted Child Today* 24, no. 1 (2001): 14–15.

————. *Once Upon a Mind: The Stories and Scholars of Gifted Child Education* (Fort Worth, TX: Harcourt, Brace, 2000).

————. "Profoundly Gifted Guilt." *Communicator* 32, no. 1 (2001).

————. "Tips for Parents: Socialization and the Profoundly Gifted Child" (online). Reno, NV: Davidson Institute for Talent Development, 2002 (cited 9 April 2003). Available at http://www.ditd.org/cybersource/record.aspx?sid=11161&scat=902&stype=110.

Delisle, James R., and Sandra L. Berger. "Underachieving Gifted Students." *ERIC Clearinghouse on Handicapped and Gifted Children* (1990), ERIC #E478.

Delisle, James R., and Judy Galbraith. *When Gifted Kids Don't Have All the Answers* (Minneapolis, MN: Free Spirit Publishing, 2002).

DeLong, Mark. "University-Based Talent Searches for the Gifted." *Understanding Our Gifted* 6, no. 4 (1994): 11–14.

D'Epiro, Peter, and Mary Desmond Pinkowish. *Sprezzatura: 50 Ways Italian Geniuses Shaped the World* (New York: Random House, 2001).

de Tocqueville, Alexis. "Why the Americans Are More Addicted to Practical than to Theoretical Science." In *Democracy in America,* trans. by Henry Reeve (New York: Longmans, Green, 1889).

Detterman, Douglas, and Joanne Ruthsatz. "The Importance of Individual Differences for Exceptional Achievement." In *Talent Development*, vol. 4, ed. by Nicholas Colangelo and Susan Assouline (Scottsdale, AZ: Great Potential Press, 2001), pp. 135–53.

Dixon, Felicia, and Cheryll Adams, eds. *2001 Research Briefs,* vol. 15 (Waco, TX: Prufrock Press, 2001).

"Dr. William Sack's Evaluation of Kinkel" (online). PBS Online and WGBH/Frontline, 2000 (cited 7 April 2003). Available at http://www.pbs.org/wgbh/pages/frontline/shows/kinkel/trial/sack.html.

Dunham, William. *Journey Through Genius: The Great Theorems of Mathematics.* (New York: John Wiley, 1990).

Durden, William G., and Arne E. Tangherlini. *Smart Kids: How Academic Talents Are Developed and Nurtured in America* (Seattle, WA: Hogrefe & Huber, 1994).

Eckstein, Peter. "The Childhood of a Computer Pioneer—Jay Forrester." In Nicholas Colangelo, Susan Assouline, DeAnn Ambroson, eds., *Talent Development* (Dayton, OH: Ohio Psychology Press, 1994).

Eilber, Charles R. "The North Carolina School of Science and Mathematics." *Phi Delta Kappan 68* (June 1987): 773–77.

Eisner, Elliot W. "The Uses and Limits of Performance Assessment" (online). *Phi Delta Kappan* 80, no. 9 (May 1999) (cited 1 August 2003). Available at http://www.pdkintl.org/kappan/keis9905.htm.

Elkind, David. "Acceleration," *Young Children* 43, no. 4 (May 1988): 2.

Emerick, Linda J. "Academic Underachievement Among the Gifted: Students' Perceptions of Factors That Reverse the Pattern." *Gifted Child Quarterly* 36, no. 3 (1992): 140–46.

Engle, Shaena. "College Freshmen Spend Less Time Studying and More Time Surfing the Net, UCLA Survey Reveals" (online). Higher Education Research Institute, UCLA Graduate School of Education and Information Studies, 2003 (cited 4 April 2003). Available at http://www.gseis.ucla.edu/heri/02_press_release.pdf.

English, Bella. "Brightest Students Lose Out." *Boston Globe,* 20 October 2002, p. 4.

Espenshade, Linda. "Extremely Gifted Kids Search for New Challenges: With an IQ Measurement Off the Chart, It Can Be Tough to Find Your Own Place." *Intelligencer Journal,* 22 August 2002, p. AA1.

Eysenck, Hans. *Genius: The Natural History of Creativity.* In *Problems in the Behavioral Sciences,* 2nd ed., ed. by Jeffrey Gray (Cambridge, Eng.: Cambridge University Press, 1995).

Feldhusen, John F. "Motivating Academically Able Youth with Enriched and Accelerated Learning Experiences." In *Intellectual Talent,* ed. by Camilla Persson Benbow and David Lubinski (Baltimore, MD: Johns Hopkins University Press, 1996), pp. 145–58.

Feldhusen, John F., ed. *Toward Excellence in Gifted Education* (Denver, CO: Love Publishing, 1985).

Feldhusen, John F., and Fathi A. Jarwan. "Identification of Gifted and Talented Youth for Educational Programs." In *International Handbook of Giftedness and Talent,* ed. by Kurt A. Heller et al. (Amsterdam: Elsevier Science, 2000).

Feldhusen, John F., and Sidney M. Moon. "Grouping Gifted Students: Issues and Concerns." *Gifted Child Quarterly* 36, no. 2 (1992): 63–67.

Feldhusen, John F., Theron Procter, and Katheryn Black. "Guidelines for Grade Advancement of Precocious Children." *Roeper Review* 9, no. 1 (1986): 25–27.

Feldman, David Henry. "A Follow-Up of Subjects Scoring Above 180 IQ." *Exceptional Children* 50, no. 6 (1984): 518–23.

———. "Child Prodigies: A Distinctive Form of Giftedness." *Gifted Child Quarterly* 37, no. 4 (1993): 188–93.

———. "Extreme Giftedness: A Developmental View." In *Talent Development: Proceedings from the 1991 Henry B. and Jocelyn Wallace National Research Symposium on Talent Development,* ed. by Nicholas Colangelo, Susan Assouline, and DeAnn Ambroson (Melbourne, Australia: Hawker Brownlow, 1992).

———. "The Mysterious Case of Extreme Giftedness." In *The Gifted and the Talented: Their Education and Development,* ed. by A. Harry Passow (Chicago: University of Chicago Press, 1979), pp. 335–51.

———. *Nature's Gambit: Child Prodigies and the Development of Human Potential,* ed. by James H. Borland (New York: Teachers College Press, 1991).

Feldman, David Henry, and Jane Piirto. "Parenting Talented Children." In *Handbook of Parenting,* ed. by Marc H. Bornstein (New York: Longman, 1995), pp. 285–304.

Fiedler, Ellen D. "Foundations for Understanding the Social-Emotional Needs of the Highly Gifted." *Highly Gifted Children* 12, no. 1 (1998): 2–5, 10.

Fiedler, Ellen D., Richard E. Lange, and Susan Winebrenner. "In Search of Reality: Unraveling the Myths About Tracking, Ability Grouping, and the Gifted." *Roeper Review* 16 (2002): 108–18.

Flanders, James R. "How Much of the Content in Mathematics Textbooks Is New?" *Arithmetic Teacher* (1987): 18–22.

Flynn, James R. "The Mean IQ of Americans: Massive Gains 1932–1978." *Psychological Bulletin* 95 (1984): 29–51.

———. "Searching for Justice: The Discovery of IQ Gains Over Time." *American Psychologist* 54, no. 1 (1999): 5–20.

Fox, Lynn H., and Jerrilene Washington. "Programs for the Gifted and Talented: Past, Present, and Future." In *The Gifted and Talented: Developmental Perspectives,* ed. by Francis Degen Horowitz and Marion O'Brian (Washington, DC: American Psychological Association, 1985), pp. 197–221.

Friedman, Reva C., and Karen B. Rogers. *Talent in Context: Historical and Social Perspectives on Giftedness* (Washington, DC: American Psychological Association, 1998).

Gagné, Francoys. "Transforming Gifts into Talents: The DMGT as a Developmental Theory." In *Handbook of Gifted Education,* ed. by Nicholas Colangelo and Gary Davis (Boston: Allyn and Bacon, 2003), pp. 60–74.

———. "When IQ Is Controlled, Does Motivation Still Predict Achievement?" *Intelligence* 30 (2000): 71–100.

Galbraith, Judy. "The Eight Great Gripes of Gifted Kids: Responding to Special Needs," *Roeper Review* 8, no. 1 (1985): 15–18.

———. *The Gifted Kids Survival Guide (for Ages 10 and Under)* (Minneapolis, MN: Free Spirit Publishing, 1984).

Gailbraith, Judy, and James Delisle. *The Gifted Kids Survival Guide: A Teen Handbook* (Minneapolis, MN: Free Spirit Publishing, 1996).

Gallagher, James J. "Comments on 'the Reform Without Cost?'" *Phi Delta Kappan* 77, no. 3 (1995): 216–17.

———. "Educational Research and Educational Policy: The Strange Case of Acceleration." In *Intellectual Talent: Psychometric and Social Issues,* ed. by Camilla Benbow and David Lubinski (Baltimore, MD: Johns Hopkins University Press, 1996), pp. 83–92.

———. "Issues and Challenges in the Education of Gifted Students." In *Handbook of Gifted Education,* ed. by Nicholas Colangelo and Gary Davis (Boston: Allyn and Bacon, 2003).

———. "National Agenda for Educating Gifted Students: Statement of Priorities." *Exceptional Children* 55, no. 2 (1988): 107–14.

———. "Society's Role in Educating Gifted Students: The Role of Public Policy." (Storrs: National Research Center on the Gifted and Talented, University of Connecticut, 2002).

———. "Unthinkable Thoughts: Education of Gifted Students." *Gifted Child Quarterly* 44, no. 1 (2000): 5–12.

Gallagher, James J., and Shelagh A. Gallagher. *Teaching the Gifted Child,* 4th ed. (Boston: Allyn and Bacon, 1994).

Gallagher, James, Christine C. Harradine, and Mary R. Coleman. "Challenge or Boredom? Gifted Students' Views on Their Schooling." *Roeper Review* 19, no. 3 (1997): 132–36.

Gamoran, Adam, and Matthew Weinstein. "Differentiation and Opportunity in Restructured Schools." *American Journal of Education* 106 (1998): 132–36.

Gardner, Howard. *Extraordinary Minds, Masterminds* (New York: Basic Books, 1997).

———. *Frames of Mind: The Theory of Multiple Intelligences,* 10th ed. (New York: Basic Books, 1993).

———. "Six Afterthoughts: Comments on 'Varieties of Intellectual Talents.'" *Journal of Creative Behaviors* 31, no. 2 (1997): 120–24.

Gardner, John. *Excellence: Can We Be Equal and Excellent Too?* rev. ed. (New York: W. W. Norton, 1995).

Geiger, Rebecca. "Nurturing for Wisdom and Compassion: Influencing Those Who Influence." In *Talent Development,* vol. 4, ed. by Nicholas Colangelo and Susan Assouline (Scottsdale, AZ: Great Potential Press, 2001), pp. 345–49.

Ginsburg, Gina. *How to Help Your Gifted Child: A Handbook for Parents and Teachers* (New York: Monarch Press, 1977).

Goertzel, Victor, and Mildred G. Goertzel. *Cradles of Eminence: A Provocative Study of the Childhoods of Over 400 Famous Twentieth-Century Men and Women* (Boston: Little, Brown, 1962).

Goldsmith, Lynn T. "Girl Prodigies: Some Evidence and Some Speculations." *Roeper Review* 10, no. 2 (1987): 74–82.

Goldstein, D., and H. Wagner. "After-School Programs, Competitions, School Olympics and Summer Programs." In *International Handbook of Research and Development of Giftedness and Talent*, ed. by Kurt Heller, Franz Monks, and A. Henry Passow (Oxford, Eng.: Pergamon, 1993), 593–604.

Goleman, Daniel. "1528 Little Geniuses and How They Grew." *Psychology Today* 13, no. 9 (1980): 28–53.

Gorden, Edward, and Alexander Thomas. "Children's Behavioral Style and the Teacher's Appraisal of Their Intelligence." *Journal of School Psychology* 5, no. 4 (1967): 292–300.

Gottfredson, Linda S. "Mainstream Science on Intelligence: An Editorial with 52 Signatories, History, and Bibliography." *Intelligence* 24, no. 1 (1997): 25–52.

———. "The Science and Politics of Intelligence in Gifted Education." In *Handbook of Gifted Education*, ed. by Nicholas Colangelo and Gary Davis (Boston: Allyn and Bacon, 2003), pp. 24–40.

Gross, Miraca. "The Early Development of Three Profoundly Gifted Children of 200 IQ." In *To Be Young and Gifted*, ed. by Pnina S. Klein and Abraham J. Tannenbaum (Norwood, NJ: Ablex Publishing, 1992).

———. *Exceptionally Gifted Children* (New York: Routledge, 1993).

———. "Exceptionally and Profoundly Gifted Students: An Underserved Population." *Understanding Our Gifted* 12, no. 2 (2000): 3–9.

———. "Factors in the Social Adjustment and Social Acceptability of Extremely Gifted Children." In *Talent Development*, vol. 2, ed. by Nicholas Colangelo and Susan Assouline (Dayton, OH: Ohio Psychology Press, 1994).

———. "From 'Play Partner' to 'Sure Shelter': How Conceptions of Friendship Differ Between Average Ability, Moderately Gifted, and Highly Gifted Children." Paper presented at the Fifth Wallace National Research Symposium on Talent Development, University of Iowa, 19 May 2000.

———. "Issues in the Cognitive Development of Exceptionally and Profoundly Gifted Individuals." In *International Handbook of Giftedness and Talent*, ed. by Kurt A. Heller et al. (Amsterdam: Elsevier Science, 2000), pp. 179–92.

———. "The 'Me' Behind the Mask: Intellectually Gifted Students and the Search for Identity." *Roeper Review* 20, no. 3 (1998): 167–74.

———. "Musings: Gifted Children and the Gift of Friendship." *Understanding Our Gifted* 14, no. 3 (2002): 27–29.

———. "The Pursuit of Excellence or the Search for Intimacy? The Forced Choice Dilemma of Gifted Youth." *Roeper Review* 11, no. 4 (1989): 189–94.

———. "Radical Acceleration: Responding to Academic and Social Needs of Extremely Gifted Adolescents." *The Journal of Secondary Gifted Education* 4, no. 4 (1994).

———. "Small Poppies: Highly Gifted Children in the Early Years." *Roeper Review* 21, no. 3 (1999): 207–14.

———. "Social and Emotional Issues for Exceptionally Intellectually Gifted Students." In *The Social and Emotional Development of Gifted Children: What Do We Know?* ed. by Maureen Niehart et al. (Waco, TX: Prufrock Press, 2002), pp. 19–29.

———. "The Use of Radical Acceleration in Cases of Extreme Intellectual Precocity." *Gifted Child Quarterly* 36, no. 2 (1992): 91–99.

———. *What Research Tells Us . . . About Ensuring the Success of Your School's Gifted Programs: Dr. Joyce Van Tassel-Baska.* GERRIC (Gifted Education Research Resource and Information Centre, Sydney, NSW, Austrailia), 2000. Audiotape.

———. *What Research Tells Us . . . About How Ability Grouping Affects Gifted Students' Self-Esteem.* GERRIC (Gifted Education Resource and Information Centre, Sydney, NSW, Australia), 2000. Audiotape.

———. *What Research Tells Us . . . About Parenting Gifted and Talented Students: Dr. Donna Enersen.* GERRIC, 2000. Audiotape.

———. *What Research Tells Us . . . About Planning and Implementing Programs for the Gifted: Dr. James Borland.* GERRIC, 2000. Audiotape.

Hanninen, Gail E. "A Study of Teacher Training in Gifted Education." *Roeper Review* 10, no. 3 (1988): 139–44.

Hansen, J. B., and John F. Feldhusen. "Comparison of Trained and Untrained Teachers of Gifted Students." *Gifted Child Quarterly* 38, no. 3 (1994): 115–21.

Heacox, Diane. *Up from Underachievement* (Minneapolis, MN: Free Spirit Publishing, 1991).

Heller, Kurt A., et al., eds. *International Handbook of Giftedness and Talent*, 2nd ed. (Amsterdam: Elsevier Science, 2000).

Henderson, Shelia J., Nancy E. Jackson, and A. Muckamal. "Early Development of Language and Literacy Skills of an Extremely Precocious Reader." *Gifted Child Quarterly* 37, no. 2 (1993).

Henry, William A., III. *In Defense of Elitism* (New York: Anchor Books, 1994).

Hofstadter, Richard. *Anti-Intellectualism in American Life* (New York: Vintage, 1962).

Hollingworth, Leta. *Children Above 180 IQ* (North Stratford, NH: Ayer Company Publishers, 1942).

———. "What We Know About the Early Selection and Training of Leaders." *Teachers College Record* 40 (1939): 575–92.

Howe, Michael J. A. *The Psychology of High Abilities* (New York: New York University Press, 1999).

Howley, Craig, Aimee Howley, and Edwina D. Pendarvis. "Out of Our Minds: Anti-Intellectualism and Talent Development in American Schooling." In James H. Borland, ed., *Education and Psychology of the Gifted* (New York: Teachers College Press, 1995).

Humphreys, Lloyd G., "A Conceptualization of Intellectual Giftedness." In *The Gifted and Talented: Developmental Perspectives*, ed. by F. D. Horowitz and M. O'Brien (Washington, DC: American Psychological Association, 1985), pp. 331–60.

Janos, Paul M., Kristi Marwood, and Nancy Robinson. "Friendship Patterns in Highly Intelligent Children." *Roeper Review* 8, no. 1 (1985): 46–49.

Janos, Paul M., and Nancy Robinson. "Performance of Students in a Program of Radical Acceleration at the University Level." *Gifted Child Quarterly* 29, no. 4 (1985): 175–79.

———. "Psychosocial Development in Intellectually Gifted Children." In *The Gifted and Talented: Developmental Perspectives*, ed. by F. D. Horowitz and M. O'Brien (Washington, DC: American Psychological Association, 1985), pp. 197–221.

Janos, Paul M., Nancy Robinson, and Clifford E. Lunneborg. "Markedly Early Entrance to College." *Journal of Higher Education* 60, no. 5 (1989): 495–518.

Janos, Paul M., et al. "A Cross-Sectional Developmental Study of the Social Relations of Students Who Enter College Early." *Gifted Child Quarterly* 32, no. 1 (1988). Available at http://www.gt-cybersource.org.

Jones, John Hodge, et al. "Prisoners of Time: Report of the National Education Commission on Time and Learning" (Washington, DC: National Education Commission, 1994).

Kanigel, Robert. *Apprentice to Genius—the Making of a Scientific Dynasty* (New York: Macmillan, 1986).

Kantrowitz, Barbara, and Debra Rosenberg. "In a Class of Their Own: For Exceptionally Gifted Children, the Best School Can Be the One at Home." *Newsweek*, 10 January 1994, p. 58.

Kariya, Takehiko, and James E. Rosenbaum. "Bright Flight: Unintended Consequences of Detracking Policy in Japan." *American Journal of Education* 107 (May 1999): 210–30.

Karnes, Frances A., and Ronald G. Marquardt. *Gifted Children and Legal Issues in Education: Parents' Stories of Hope* (Scottsdale, AZ: Gifted Psychology Press, 1991).

———. *Gifted Children and the Law: Mediation, Due Process, and Court Cases* (Scottsdale, AZ: Gifted Psychology Press, 1991).

Karnes, Francis A., Kristin R. Stephens, and James E. Whorton. "Certification and Specialized Competencies for Teachers in Gifted Education Programs." *Roeper Review* 22, no. 3 (2000): 201–2.

Kaufmann, Felice. "What Educators Can Learn from Gifted Adults." In *Talent for the Future,* ed. by Franz Monks and W. Peters (Assen: The Netherlands: Van Gorcum, 1992).

Kaufmann, Felice, M. Layne Kalbfleisch, and F. Xavier Castellanos. "Attention Deficit Disorders and Gifted Students: What Do We Really Know?" (Storrs: The National Research Center on the Gifted and Talented, University of Connecticut, 2000) pp. 6–13.

Kay, Kiesa. "An Anomaly: Parenting a Twice Exceptional Girl." *Highly Gifted Children* 12, no. 2 (1998). Available at http://www.ditd.org/cybersource/record.aspx?sid=11498&scat=902&stype=110.

Kearney, Kathi. "Discriminating Against Excellence." *Understanding Our Gifted* (1993).

———. "Early Signs of Extreme Intelligence" (online). Reno, NV: Davidson Institute for Talent Development (cited 9 April 2003). Available at http://www.gt-cybersource.org.

———. "Highly Gifted Children in Full Inclusion Classrooms." *Highly Gifted Children* 12, no. 4 (1996): 159–66.

———. "Life in the Asynchronous Family." *Understanding Our Gifted* 4, no. 6 (1992): 1, 8–12.

———. "Parenting Highly Gifted Children: The Challenges, the Joys, the Unexpected Surprises." *CAG Communicator* 19, no. 2 (1989).

Kerr, Barbara, and Nicholas Colangelo. "Something to Prove: Academically Talented Minority Students." In *Talent Development*, vol. 2, ed. by Nicholas Colangelo, Susan Assouline, and DeAnn Ambroson (Dayton, OH: Ohio Psychology Press, 1994).

Kerr, Barbara, Nicholas Colangelo, and Julie Gaeth. "Gifted Adolescents' Attitudes Toward Their Giftedness." *Gifted Child Quarterly* 32, no. 2 (1988): 245–47.

Kim, Scott. "Bogglers." *Discover* 24, no. 6 (June 2003): 80.

Knope, Muriel. "Homeschooling: An Accidental Journey." *Ohio Association for Gifted Children Review* (2002).

Kolloff, Penny B. "State-Supported Residential High Schools." In *Handbook of Gifted Education*, ed. by Nicholas Colangelo and Gary Davis (Boston: Allyn and Bacon, 2003), pp. 238–46.

Kottmeyer, Carolyn. "The Internet and the Highly Gifted Child." *Communicator* 31, no. 4 (2000). Available at http://www.gt-cybersource.org.

Kozol, Jonathan. *Savage Inequalities: Children in America's Schools* (New York: Harper, 1992).

Kulik, James A. *An Analysis of the Research on Ability Grouping: Historical and Contemporary Perspectives* (Storrs: National Research Center on the Gifted and Talented, University of Connecticut, 1992).

———. "Grouping and Tracking." In *Handbook of Gifted Education*, ed. by Nicholas Colangelo and Gary A. Davis (Boston: Pearson Education, 2003), pp. 268–81.

Kulik, James A., and Chen-Lin C. Kulik. "The Effects of Accelerated Instruction on Students." *Review of Educational Research* 54, no. 3 (1984): 409–25.

———. "Synthesis of Research on Effects of Accelerated Instruction." *Educational Leadership* 42 (1984): 84–89.

Kunkel, Mark A., et al. "Experience of Giftedness 'Eight Great Gripes' Six Years Later." *Roeper Review* 15, no. 1 (1992): 10–14.

Levine, Mel. *A Mind at a Time.* (New York: Simon & Schuster, 2002).

Linchevski, Liora, and Bilha Kutscher. "Tell Me with Whom You're Learning, and I'll Tell You How Much You've Learned: Mixed-Ability Versus Same-Ability Grouping in Mathematics." *Journal for Research in Mathematics Education* 29, no. 5 (1998): 533–54.

Lind, Sharon. "Before Referring a Gifted Child for ADD, ADHD Evaluation." *Communicator* 31, no. 4 (2000): 20.

———. "Overexcitability and the Highly Gifted." *Communicator* 31, no. 4 (2000): 19, 45–48.

———. "Tips for Parents: Introverts" (online). Reno, NV: Davidson Institute for Talent Development, 2002 (cited 9 April 2003). Available at http://www.gt-cybersource.org.

Link, Frances R., ed. *Essays on the Intellect* (Alexandria, VA: Association for Supervision and Curriculum Development, 1985).

Lockwood, John H., and Ella F. Cleveland. "The Challenge of Detracking: Finding the Balance Between Equity and Excellence" (online). Association of American Medical Colleges Community and Minority Programs, 12 November 2002 (cited 9 April 2003). Available at http://eric-web.tc.columbia.edu/npinpdfs/detracking. pdf.

Lovecky, Deirdre V. "Exceptionally Gifted Children: Different Minds." *Roeper Review* 17, no. 2 (1994): 116–20.

———. "Exploring Social and Emotional Aspects of Giftedness in Children." *Roeper Review* 15, no. 1 (1992): 18–25.

———. "Hidden Gifted Learner." *Understanding Our Gifted* (March/April 1992): 3–4.

———. "Highly Gifted Children with Attention Deficit Disorder." *Highly Gifted Children* 7, no. 2 (1991).

———. "Highly Gifted Children and Peer Relations." *Counseling and Guidance Newsletter* 5, no. 3 (1995): 2, 6–7.

Loveless, Tom. *The Tracking Wars: State Reform Meets School Policy* (Washington, DC: Brookings Institution Press, 1999), 1–40.

———. *The Tracking and Ability Grouping Debate* (Washington, DC: Thomas B. Fordham Foundation, 1999).

Lubinski, David, and Camilla Persson Benbow. "Optimal Development of Talent: Respond Educationally to Individual Differences in Personality." *Educational Forum* 59 (1995): 381–92.

Lubinski, David, et al. "Top 1 in 10,0000: A 10-Year Follow-Up of the Profoundly Gifted." *Journal of Applied Psychology* 86, no. 4 (2001): 718–29.

Lupkowski, Ann E., Susan Assouline, and Julian Stanley. "Beyond Testing: Applying a Mentor Model for Young Mathematically Talented Students." *Gifted Child Today* 67, no. 13 (1990): 2–4.

Lupkowski, Ann E., Susan Assouline, and J. Vestol. "Mentors in Math." *Gifted Child Today* 15, no. 3 (1992): 26–31.

Lupkowski-Shoplik, Ann E., Susan Assouline. "Evidence of Extreme Mathematical Precocity: Case Studies of Talented Youths." *Roeper Review* 16, no. 3 (1994): 144–51.

Lupkowski-Shoplik, Ann, et al. "Talent Searches: Meeting the Needs of Academically Talented Youth." In *Handbook of Gifted Education*, ed. by Nicholas Colangelo and Gary A. Davis (Boston: Allyn & Bacon, 2003), pp. 1–22.

Lupkowski-Shoplik, Ann E., Michael F. Saylor, and Susan Assouline. "Trends in Performance of Mathematically Talented Elementary Students on Out-of-Level Achievement Tests of Mathematics Computation and Basic Concepts." In *Talent Development: Proceedings for the 1993 Henry B. and Jocelyn Wallace National Research Symposium on Talent Development*, ed. by Nicholas Colangelo, Susan Assouline, and DeAnn Ambroson (Dayton, OH: Ohio Psychology Press, 1993), pp. 409–14.

Martin, Edwin W., Reed Martin, and Donna L. Terman. "The Legislative and Litigation History of Special Education." *The Future of Children* 6, no. 1 (1996): 25–39.

Mathis, William J. "No Child Left Behind: Cost and Benefits" (online). *Phi Delta Kappan* 84, no. 9 (2003) (cited 1 August 2003). Available at http://www.pdkintl.org/kappan/k0305mat.htm.

McNabb, Terry. "Motivational Issues: Potential to Performance." In *Handbook of Gifted Education*, ed. by Nicholas Colangelo and Gary Davis (Boston: Allyn and Bacon, 2003), pp. 417–23.

McNamara, Mary. "Learn, Baby, Learn." *Los Angeles Times*, 1 April 2001, p. E1.

Mead, Margaret. "The Gifted Child in the American Culture of Today." *Journal of Teacher Education* 5 (1954): 211–14.

Meckstroth, Betty. "Survival Kit for Parents of Exceptionally Gifted Children." *Highly Gifted Children* 10, no. 4 (1995): 4.

Mitchell, Valory. "La Suer Says Education Governor's Veto of AB 2626 Is a Slap in the Face to California's Highly Gifted Students" (online). California assemblyman Jay La Suer's website, 1 October 2002 (cited 4 April 2003). Available at http://republican.assembly.ca.gov/members/index.asp?Dist=77&Lang=1&Body=PressRelease&RefID=559.

Mondale, Sarah, and Sarah B. Patton, eds. *School: The Story of American Public Education* (Boston: Beacon Press, 2001).

Monks, Franz J., Kurt A. Heller, and A. Harry Passow. "The Study of Giftedness: Reflections on Where We Are and Where We Are Going." In *International Handbook of Giftedness and Talent*, ed. by Kurt A. Heller et al. (Amsterdam: Elsevier Science, 2000), pp. 839–63.

Moon, Sidney. "Developing Personal Talent." Paper presented at the Eighth Annual Conference of the European Council for High Ability, Rhodes, Greece, October 2002.

Moon, Sidney M., Joan A. Jurich, and John F. Feldhusen. "Families of Gifted Children: Cradles of Development." In *Talent in Context: Historical and Social Perspectives on Giftedness*, ed. by Reva C. Friedman and Karen B. Rogers (Washington, DC: American Psychological Association, 1998), pp. 81–99.

Moon, Sidney M., and Hilda C. Rosselli. "Developing Gifted Programs." In *International Handbook of Giftedness and Talent*, ed. by Kurt A. Heller et al. (Amsterdam: Elsevier Science, 2000), pp. 499–521.

Morelock, Martha. "Giftedness: The View from Within." *Understanding Our Gifted* 4, no. 3 (1992): 1, 11–15.

Morelock, Martha, and David Feldman. "Extreme Precocity." In *Handbook of Gifted Education*, ed. by Nicholas Colangelo and Gary Davis (Boston: Allyn and Bacon, 1997).

Morris, Bonnie Rotham. "Home Schooling in CyberSpace." *New York Times*, 29 May 2003.

Mosteller, Fredrick, Richard J. Light, and Jason A. Sachs. "Sustained Inquiry in Education: Lessons from Skill Grouping and Class Size." *Harvard Educational Review* 66, no. 4 (1996): 797–842.

Murray, Penelope, ed. *Genius: The History of an Idea* (Oxford, Eng.: Basil Blackwell, 1989).

National Council for Teachers of English, "Tracked for Failure/Tracked for Success" (online). Urbana, IL: National Council for Teachers of English (cited 2 April 2003). Available at http://www.ncte.org/about/over/positions/level/elem/107685.htm.

Neihart, Maureen. "Creativity, the Arts and Madness." *Roeper Review* 21, no. 1 (1998): 47–50.

_____. "Gifted Children with Asperger's Syndrome." *Gifted Child Quarterly* 44, no. 4 (2000): 222–30.

_____. "The Impact of Giftedness on Psychological Well-Being." *Roeper Review* 22, no. 1 (1999).

Neihart, Maureen, and F. Richard Olenchak. "Creatively Gifted Children." In *The Social and Emotional Development of Gifted Children: What Do We Know?* ed. by Maureen Neihart et al. (Waco, TX: Prufrock Press, 2002), pp. 165–75.

Neihart, Maureen, et al., eds. *The Social and Emotional Development of Gifted Children: What Do We Know?* (Waco, TX: Prufrock Press, 2002).

Neville, Christine. "Portfolio—an Effective Way to Present Your Child to the School." *Highly Gifted Children* 11, no. 1 (1997).

"The 1998–1999 State of the States Gifted and Talented Education Report" (Longmont, CO: Council of State Directors of Programs of the Gifted, 2001).

Noble, Kathleen, and Julie Drummond. "But What About the Prom?" *Gifted Child Quarterly* 36, no. 4 (1992): 106–11.

Noble, Kathleen, Nancy Robinson, and Susan Gunderson. "All Rivers Lead to the Sea: A Follow-Up Study of Gifted Young Adults." *Roeper Review* 15, no. 3 (1993): 124–30.

Noble, Kathleen, Rena F. Subotnik, and Karen D. Arnold. "To Thine Own Self Be True: A New Model of Female Talent Development." *Gifted Child Quarterly* 43, no. 4 (1999): 140–49.

Noble, Kathleen, et al. "Different Strokes: Perceptions of Social and Emotional Development Among Early College Entrants." *Journal of Secondary Gifted Education* 10, no. 2 (1998/1999): 77–84.

Norton, John, and Ann Lewis. "Middle-Grades Reform." *Kappan* 81, no. 10 (2000): K1.

Oakes, Jeannie. *Keeping Track: How Schools Structure Inequality* (New Haven, CT: Yale University Press, 1985).

Oakes, Jeannie, Kevin Welner, and Susan Yonezawa. *Mandating Equity: A Case Study of Court-Ordered Detracking in the San Jose Schools* (Berkeley: California Policy Seminar's Policy Research Program, 1998).

Ochse, R. A. *Before the Gates of Excellence: The Determinants of Creative Genius* (Cambridge, Eng.: Cambridge University Press, 1990).

Oden, M. "A Forty-Year Follow-Up of Giftedness: Fulfillment and Unfulfillment." In *Genius & Eminence: The Social Psychology of Creativity and*

Exceptional Achievement, ed. by Robert S. Albert (Oxford, Eng.: Pergamon Press, 1983), pp. 203–13.

Okagaki, Lynn, and Peter A. Frensch. "Parenting and Children's Achievement: A Multiethnic Perspective." *American Educational Research Journal* 35, no. 1 (1998): 123–44.

Olenchak, F. Richard, and Joseph S. Renzulli. "The Effectiveness of the Schoolwide Enrichment Model on Selected Aspects of Elementary School Change." *Gifted Child Quarterly* 33, no. 1 (1989): 36–46.

Olszewski-Kubilius, Paula. "Parenting Practices That Promote Talent Development, Creativity, and Optimal Adjustment." In *The Social and Emotional Development of Gifted Children: What Do We Know?* ed. by Maureen Neihart et al. (Waco, TX: Prufrock Press, 2002).

Olszewski-Kubillus, Paula, and L. Limburg-Weber. "Options for Middle School and Secondary Level Gifted Students." *Journal of Secondary Gifted Education* 11, no. 1 (1999): 4–10.

Olszewski-Kubilius, Paula, Marilynn Kulieke, and N. Krasney. "Personality Dimensions of Gifted Adolescents: A Review of the Empirical Literature." *Gifted Child Quarterly* 32, no. 4 (1988): 347–52.

Osborn, Julia B. "Gifted Children: Are Their Gifts Being Identified, Encouraged or Ignored?" (online) (cited 9 April 2003). Available at http://www.gt-cybersource.org.

——. "Issues in Educating Exceptionally Gifted Students" (online). Reno, NV: Davidson Foundation, 2001 (cited 9 April 2003). Available at http://www.www.gt-cybersource.org.

Page, Ellis B., and Timothy Z. Keith. "The Elephant in the Classroom: Ability Grouping and the Gifted." In *Intellectual Talent*, ed. by Camilla Persson Benbow and David Lubinski (Baltimore, MD: Johns Hopkins University Press, 1996), pp. 192–210.

Passow, A. Harry. "Acceleration Over the Years." In *Intellectual Talent*, ed. by Camilla Persson Benbow and David Lubinski (Baltimore, MD: Johns Hopkins University Press, 1996), pp. 93–98.

——. "Intellectual Development of the Gifted." In *Essays on the Intellect*, ed. by Frances R. Link (Alexandria, VA: Association for Supervision and Curriculum Development, 1985), pp. 23–43.

——. "National/State Policies Regarding Education of the Gifted." In *International Handbook of Research and Development of Giftedness and Talent*, ed. by Kurt A. Heller, Franz J. Monks, and A. Henry Passow (Oxford, Eng.: Pergamon, 1993), pp. 29–46.

Perleth, Cristoph, Tanja Schatz, and Franz J. Monks. "Early Identification of High Ability." In *International Handbook of Giftedness and Talent*, ed. by Kurt A. Heller et al. (Amsterdam: Elsevier Science, 2000), pp. 297–316.

Peterson, J. S., and Nicholas Colangelo. "Gifted Achievers and Underachievers: A Comparison of Patterns Found in School Files." *Journal of Counseling and Development* 74 (March/April 1996): 399–407.

Piaget, Jean. *The Child's Conception of the World* (Totowa, NJ: Littlefield, Adams, 1965).

———. *The Origins of Intelligence in Children* (New York: W. W. Norton, 1962).

Piirto, Jane. *Understanding Those Who Create*, 2d ed. (Scottsdale, AZ: Gifted Psychology Press, 1988).

Pinker, Steven. *The Blank Slate: The Modern Denial of Human Nature* (New York: Viking, 2002).

Plucker, Jonathan R. "Is Gifted Education Still Viable?" *Education Week* 17, no. 26 (1998). Available at http://www.edweek.org/ew/vol-17/26pluck.h17.

Powell, Phillip M., and Tony Haden. "The Intellectual and Psychosocial Nature of Extreme Giftedness." *Roeper Review* 6, no. 3 (1984): 131–33.

"President Bush Asks Congress for $1.8 Billion for Pennsylvania's Students" (online). Washington, DC: U.S. Department of Education, 4 February 2002 (cited 4 April 2003). Available at http://www.ed.gov/news/press releases/2002/02/state-by-state/pennsylvania.html.

"President Bush Asks Congress for $1.6 Billion for Michigan's Students" (online). Washington, DC: U.S. Department of Education, 4 February 2002 (cited 4 April 2003). Available at http://www.ed.gov/news/press releases/2002/02/state-by-state/michigan.html.

"President Bush Asks Congress for $5.8 Billion for California's Students" (online). Washington, DC: U.S. Department of Education, 4 February 2002 (cited 4 April 2003). Available at http://www.ed.gov/news/press releases/2002/02/state-by-state/california.html.

Pringle, M. L. Kellmer. *Able Misfits: The Educational and Behavior Difficulties of Intelligent Children* (London: Longman, 1970).

Program History (online). International Telementor Program (cited 1 April 2003). Available at http://www.telementor.org/itp/aboutus.cfm.

Rash, Patricia K., and April D. Miller. "A Survey of Practices for Teachers of the Gifted." *Roeper Review* 22, no. 3 (2000): 192–94.

Ratvitch, Diane. *Left Back: A Century of Battles Over School Reform* (New York: Simon & Schuster, 2000).

Ray, Brian D., *House Education Committee Hearing for HB 2560* (online). Harrisburg, PA: House Education Committee of the Commonwealth of Pennsylvania, 13 June 2002 (cited 8 April 2003). Available at http://members.truevine.net/pilgrimspage@truevine.net/BRay testimony020613.htm.

Reider, Jon. "Tips for Parents: Early College Entrance for Profoundly Gifted Students" (online). Reno, NV: Davidson Institute for Talent Development, 2002 (cited 9 April 2003). Available at http://www.ditd.org/cyber source/record.aspx?sid=11466&scat=902&stype=110.

Reis, Sally M. "Talent Ignored, Talent Diverted: The Cultural Context Underlying Giftedness in Females." *Gifted Child Quarterly* 39, no. 3 (1995): 162–70.

Reis, Sally M., and D. Betsy McCoach. "The Underachievement of Gifted Students: What Do We Know and Where Do We Go?" *Gifted Child Quarterly* 44, no. 3 (2000): 152–70.

Rimm, Sylvia. "Family Environments of Underachieving Gifted Students." *Gifted Child Quarterly* 32, no. 4 (1988): 353–95.

———. "The Pressures Bright Children Feel and Why They May Underachieve." *On Raising Kids Newsletter* (2000): 2–3.

———. "Social Adjustment and Peer Pressures for Gifted Children" (online). Reno, NV: Davidson Institute for Talent Development, 2003 (cited 7 April 2003). Available at http://www.gt-cybersource.org.

———. "Underachievement a National Epidemic." In *Handbook of Gifted Education,* ed. by Nicholas Colangelo and Gary Davis (Boston: Allyn and Bacon, 2003), 424–44.

———. *Why Bright Kids Get Poor Grades: And What You Can Do About It* (New York: Three Rivers Press, 1995).

Rimm, Sylvia, and K. J. Lovance. "The Use of Subject and Grade Skipping for the Prevention and Reversal of Underachievement." *Gifted Child Quarterly* 36, no. 2 (1992): 100–105.

Rimm, Sylvia, Sara Rimm-Kaufman, and Ilonna J. Rimm. *See Jane Win: The Rimm Report on How 1,000 Girls Became Successful Women* (New York: Three Rivers Press, 1999).

Robinson, Ann, and Sidney M. Moon. "National Study of Local and State Advocacy: A National Study of Local and State Advocacy in Gifted Education." *Gifted Child Quarterly* 47, no. 1 (Winter 2003).

Robinson, Halbert B. "A Case for Radical Acceleration: Programs of the John Hopkins University and the University of Washington." In *Acad-*

emic Precocity: Aspects of Its Development, ed. by Camilla Persson Benbow and Julian C. Stanley (Baltimore, MD: Johns Hopkins University Press, 1983), pp. 139–59.

———. "The Uncommonly Bright Child." In *The Uncommon Child,* ed. by M. Lewis and L. A. Rosenblum (New York: Plenum Press, 1981), pp. 57–81.

Robinson, Halbert B., and Nancy Robinson. "The Use of Standardized Tests with Young Gifted Children." In *To Be Young and Gifted,* ed. by Pnina S. Klein and Abraham J. Tannenbaum (Norwood, NJ: Ablex Publishing, 1992), pp. 141–70.

Robinson, Nancy M. "Acceleration as an Option for the Highly Gifted Adolescent." In *Intellectual Talent,* ed. by Camilla Persson Benbow and David Lubinski (Baltimore, MD: Johns Hopkins University Press, 1996), pp. 169–78.

———. "Giftedness in Very Young Children: How Seriously Should It Be Taken?" In *Talent Unfolding: Cognition and Development,* ed. by R. C. Friedman and B. M. Shore (Washington, DC: American Psychological Association, 2000), pp. 7–26.

———. "Individual Differences in Gifted Students' Attributions for Academic Performances." In *The Social and Emotional Development of Gifted Children: What Do We Know?* ed. by Maureen Niehart et al. (Waco, TX: Prufrock Press, 2002), pp. 61–69.

———. "Necessity Is the Mother of Invention: The Roots of Our 'System' of Providing Educational Alternatives for Gifted Students." *Journal of Secondary Gifted Education* 10, no. 3 (1999): 120–28.

———. "Two Wrongs Do Not Make a Right: Sacrificing the Needs of Academically Gifted Students Does Not Solve Society's Unsolved Problems." *Journal for the Education of the Gifted* (in press).

Robinson, Nancy, and Halbert Robinson. "The Optimal Match: Devising the Best Compromise for Highly Gifted Students." In *Developmental Approaches to Giftedness and Creativity,* ed. by David Feldman (San Francisco: Jossey-Bass, 1982), pp. 79–94.

Robinson, Nancy, E. Zigler, and James Gallagher. "Two Tails of the Normal Curve: Similarities and Differences in the Study of Mental Retardation and Giftedness." *American Psychologist* 55, no. 12 (2000): 1413–24.

Robinson, Nancy M., et al. "Social and Emotional Issues Facing Gifted and Talented Students: What Have We Learned and What Should We Do

Now?" In *The Social and Emotional Development of Gifted Children: What Do We Know?* ed. by Maureen Neihart et al. (Waco, TX: Prufrock Press, 2002), pp. 267–89.

Robinson, Nancy M., et al. "Family Factors Associated with High Academic Competence Among Former Head Start Children." *Gifted Child Quarterly* 42 (1998): 148–56.

Rodell, Wendy. "Vulnerabilities of Highly Gifted Children." *Roeper Review* 6, no. 3 (1984): 127–30.

Rogers, Karen B. "Effects of Acceleration on Gifted Learners." In *The Social and Emotional Development of Gifted Children: What Do We Know?* ed. by Maureen Niehart et al. (Waco, TX: Prufrock Press, 2002), pp. 3–12.

———. "Grouping the Gifted and Talented: Questions and Answers." *Roeper Review* 16, no. 1 (1993): 103–7.

———. "A Study of 241 Extraordinarily Gifted Children." Paper presented at the National Association for Gifted Children Forty-fourth Annual Convention, Little Rock, Arkansas, 7 November 1997.

———. "What You Might Say . . . Possible Responses from Ch 7, Program Provisions (Grouping) Within the School." In *Re-Forming Gifted Education* (Scottsdale, AZ: Great Potential Press, 2002), 262–65.

Rogers, Karen B., and Richard D. Kimpston. "The Acceleration of Students: What We Do vs. What We Know." *Educational Leadership* 50, no. 2 (October 1992): 58–61.

Ross, Arnold E. "*Quo Vadis* America?" In *Intellectual Talent*, ed. by Camilla Persson Benbow and David Lubinski (Baltimore, MD: Johns Hopkins University Press, 1996), pp. 221–24.

Ross, Pat O'Connell. *National Excellence: A Case for Developing America's Talent* (online). U.S. Department of Education, 1993 (cited 4 June 2002). Available at http://www.ed.gov/pubs/DevTalent/part1.html.

Russell, Cathy, Karen LaBonte, and Greg Russell. "Preparing for and Holding an Effective School Meeting." *Highly Gifted Children* 12, no. 4 (1999): 3–31.

Sand, Barbara Lourie. *Teaching Genius: Dorothy DeLay and the Making of a Musician* (Portland, OR: Amadeus Press, 2000), pp. 67–71.

Sapon-Shevin, Mara. *Playing Favorites: Gifted Education and the Disruption of Community* (Albany: State University of New York Press, 1994).

Schuler, Patricia A. "Perfectionism and Gifted Adolescents." *Journal of Secondary Gifted Education* 16, no. 4 (2000): 183–96.

———. "Perfectionism in Gifted Adolescents." In *The Social and Emotional Development of Gifted Children: What Do We Know?* ed. by Maureen Neihart et al. (Waco, TX: Prufrock Press, 2002), pp. 71–79.

Schultz, Robert. "Flirting with Underachievement: Hidden for a Reason." *Highly Gifted Children* 13, no. 2 (2000): 42–48.

Secret Apartheid I (online). New York: ACORN Schools Office (cited 2 April 2003). Available at http://www.acorn.org/ACORNarchives/studies/secretapartheid.

Secret Apartheid II (online). New York: ACORN Schools Office, 1997 (cited 2 April 2003). Available at http://www.acorn.org/ACORNarchives/studies/secretapartheid2.

Seligman, Dan. "The Grade-Inflation Swindle." *Forbes,* 18 March 2002, p. 1.

Shore, Bruce M., et al. *Recommended Practices in Gifted Education: A Critical Analysis* (New York: Teachers College Press, 1991).

"Secret Service Studies Shootings" (online). *60 Minutes II,* CBS News, 15 August 2000 (cited 7 April 2003). Available at http://www.cbsnews.com/stories/2000/03/14/60II/main171898.shtml.

Silverman, Linda, and Kathi Kearney. "Parents of the Extraordinarily Gifted." *Advanced Development Journal* 1 (January 1989): 41–56.

Silverman, Linda, and Linda Leviton. "Advice to Parents in Search of the Perfect Program." *Gifted Child Today* 14, no. 6 (1991): 31–34.

Simonton, Dean Keith. *Genius, Creativity, and Leadership: Historiometric Inquiries* (Cambridge, MA: Harvard University Press, 1984).

———. "Gifted Child, Genius Adult: Three Life-Span Developmental Perspectives." In *Talent in Context,* ed. by Reva C. Friedman and Karen B. Rogers (Washington, DC: American Psychological Association, 1998), pp. 151–75.

———. *Greatness: Who Makes History and Why* (New York: Guilford Press, 1994).

———. *Origins of Genius: Darwinian Perspectives on Creativity* (New York: Oxford University Press, 1999).

———. *Scientific Genius: A Psychology of Science* (Cambridge, Eng.: Cambridge University Press, 1988).

Sinclair, Esther. "Tips for Parents: Educational Advocacy" (online). Reno, NV: Davidson Institute for Talent Development, 2002 (cited 9 April 2003). Available at http://www.gt-cybersource.org.

Singal, Daniel. "The Other Crisis in American Education." *Atlantic Monthly* 268, no. 5 (1991): 59–74.

Sloane, Katheryn D. "Home Influences on Talent Development." In *Developing Talent in Young People*, ed. by Benjamin S. Bloom (New York: Ballantine, 1985), pp. 439–76.

Smith, Betty. "Gifted, Talented Students Follow Mentors' Lead." *Oklahoma Tahlequah Daily Press*, 10 February 2003.

Smith, Deborah. "Acceleration: Is Moving Ahead the Right Step?" *Monitor on Psychology* 34, no. 5 (May 2003): 63.

———. "Cultivating Untapped Potential: Psychologists Are Developing Programs to Identify Gifted Children Earlier—and to Ensure Their Success." *Monitor on Psychology* 34, no. 5 (May 2003): 62.

Smith, Terrence. *A Conversation with Lee Cullum* (online). Online NewsHour, 31 March 2000 (cited 13 August 2002). Available at http://www.pbs.org/newshour/gergen/jan-june00/cullum_3-31.html.

Smutney, Joan Franklin. "Early Gifts, Early School Recognition." *Understanding Our Gifted* 11, no. 2 (1999): 1, 13–16.

———. "Gifted Girls." *Understanding Our Gifted* 11, no. 2 (1999): 9–13.

———. *Stand Up for Your Gifted Child* (Minneapolis, MN: Free Spirit Publishing, 2001).

Sorokin, Ellen. "Blacks Turn to Home Schooling." *Washington Times*, 9 February 2003. Available at http://rambleman.tripod.com/blacks_turn_to_homeschooling.htm.

Sosniak, Lauren A., and Judith A. Monsaas. *Developing Talent in Young People*, ed. by Benjamin S. Bloom (New York: Ballantine Books, 1985).

Stanley, Gregory Kent. "Faith Without Works? Twenty-five Years of Undervaluing Content Area Knowledge." *Educational Horizons* (Fall 2001): 24–27.

Stanley, Gregory Kent, and Lawrence Baines. "Celebrating Mediocrity: How Schools Short-Change Gifted Students." *Roeper Review* 25, no. 1 (Fall 2002): 11–13.

Stanley, Julian. "Helping Students Learn Only What They Don't Already Know." In *Talent Development*, ed. by Nicholas Colangelo and Susan Assouline (Scottsdale, AZ: Great Potential Press, 2001), pp. 293–99.

Stanley, Julian, Ann E. Lupkowski, and Susan Assouline. "Acceleration and Enrichment for Mathematically Talented Youth: Eight Considerations." *Gifted Child Today* 67, no. 13 (1990): 15–19.

Stanley, Julian, Alexander Plotinck, and Michele Cargain. "Educational Trajectories." *Gifted Child Today* 19, no. 2 (1996): 18–21, 38–39.

Stanley, Julian C., and A. M. McGill. "More About Young Entrants to College: How Did They Fare?" *Gifted Child Quarterly* 30, no. 2 (1986): 70–77.

Stein, M. I., and S. J. Heinze. "A Summary of Terman's Genetic Studies of Genius Vols. 1 and 2." In *Genius and Eminence: The Social Psychology of Creativity and Exceptional Achievement*, ed. by R. S. Albert (Oxford, Eng.: Pergamon Press, 1983), pp. 75–84.

Steptoe, Andrew, ed. *Genius and the Mind* (New York: Oxford University Press, 1998).

Sternberg, Robert. "Critical Thinking: Its Nature, Measurement, and Improvement." In *Essays on the Intellect*, ed. by Frances R. Link (Alexandria, VA: Association for Supervision and Curriculum Development, 1985), pp. 45–65.

Sternberg, Robert, ed. *Handbook of Creativity* (Cambridge, Eng.: Cambridge University Press, 1999).

Sternberg, Robert, and Joseph Horvath. "Cognitive Conceptions of Expertise and Their Relations to Giftedness." In *Talent in Context*, ed. by Reva C. Friedman and Karen B. Rogers (Washington, DC: American Psychological Association, 1998), pp. 177–91.

Sternberg, Robert, and Todd I. Lubart. "Creative Giftedness: A Multivariate Investment Approach." *Gifted Child Quarterly* 37, no. 1 (1993): 7–15.

Stevenson, Harold. "Cultural Interpretations of Giftedness: The Case of East Asia." In *Talent in Context*, ed. by Reva C. Friedman and Karen B. Rogers (Washington, DC: American Psychological Association, 1998), pp. 61–77.

Subotnik, Rena F. "Factors from the Structure of Intellect Model Associated with Gifted Adolescents' Problem Finding in Science: Research with Westinghouse Science Talent Search Winners." *Journal of Creative Behaviors* 22, no. 1 (1988): 42–54.

Subotnik, Rena F., and Karen D. Arnold, eds. *Beyond Terman: Contemporary Longitudinal Studies of Giftedness and Talent* (Norwood, NJ: Ablex Publishing, 1994).

Subotnik, Rena F., and James Borland. "Family Factors in the Adult Success of High IQ Children." *Illinois Council for the Gifted Journal* 11 (1992): 37–42.

Subotnik, Rena F., David E. Karp, and Elizabeth R. Morgan. "High-IQ Children at Midlife: An Investigation into the Generalizability of Terman's 'Genetic Studies of Genius.'" *Roeper Review* 11, no. 3 (1989): 139–44.

Subotnik, Rena F., and Cynthia L. Steiner. "Problem Identification in Academic Research: A Longitudinal Case Study from Adolescence to Early Adulthood." In *Problem Finding, Problem Solving, and Creativity*, ed. by Mark A. Runco (Norwood, NJ: Ablex Publishing, 1994), pp. 188–200.

Subotnik, Rena F., Karen Mauer Stone, and Cynthia Steiner. "Lost Generation of Elite Talent in Science." *Journal of Secondary Gifted Education* 13, no. 1 (2001): 33–44.

Swiatek, Mary Ann. "Accelerated Students' Self-Esteem and Self-Perceived Personality Characteristics: A Five-Year Longitudinal Study." *Journal of Secondary Gifted Education* 5, no. 4 (1994): 35–41.

———. "An Empirical Investigation of the Social Coping Strategies Used by Gifted Adolescents." *Gifted Child Quarterly* 39 (1995): 154–61.

———. "Tips for Parents: Social Experiences of Gifted Adolescents" (online). Reno, NV: Davidson Institute for Talent Development, 2002 (cited 9 April 2003). Available at http://www.gt-cybersource.org.

Sykes, Charles J. *Dumbing Down Our Kids: Why American Children Feel Good About Themselves but Can't Read, Write, or Add* (New York: St. Martin's Press, 1995).

Tannenbaum, Abraham J. "Bill of Rights for Gifted." In *Gifted Children: Psychological and Educational Perspectives*, ed. by Abraham J. Tannebaum (New York: Macmillan, 1983).

———. *Gifted Children: Psychological and Educational Perspectives* (New York: Macmillan, 1983).

———. "The IQ Controversy and the Gifted." In *Intellectual Talent*, ed. by Camilla Persson Benbow and David Lubinski (Baltimore, MD: Johns Hopkins University Press, 1996), pp. 44–82.

———. "Nature and Nurture of Giftedness." In *Handbook of Gifted Education*, ed. by Nicholas Colangelo and Gary Davis (Boston: Allyn and Bacon, 2003), pp. 45–59.

Tieso, Carol L. "Academic Decathlon and Secondary Students." *National Resource Center for the Gifted and Talented Newsletter* (Winter 1998).

Tofler, Ian, and Theresa Foy DiGeronimo. *Keeping Your Kids Out Front Without Kicking Them from Behind* (San Francisco: Jossey-Bass, 2000).

Tolan, Stephanie. *Is It a Cheetah?* (online). Hollingworth Center, 1997 (cited 29 May 2002). Available at http://www.ditd.org/cybersource/record.aspx?sid=11469&scat=902&stype=110.

Tomlinson, Carol Ann. "Proficiency Is Not Enough." *Education Week* 22, no. 10 (6 November 2002): 36, 38.

Tomlinson-Keasey, Carol. "Tracing the Lives of Gifted Women." In *Talent in Context*, ed. by Reva C. Friedman and Karen B. Rogers (Washington, DC: American Psychological Association, 1998), pp. 17–38.

Traub, James. "Multiple Intelligence Disorder." *The New Republic* (26 October 1998): 20–23.

Tucker, Brook, and Norma L. Hafenstein. "Psychological Intensities in Young Gifted Children." *Gifted Child Quarterly* 41, no. 3 (1997): 66–75.

Vail, Priscilla. *Smart Kids with School Problems: Things to Know and Ways to Help* (New York: New American Library, 1989).

Vanderkam, Laura. "SAT Talent Searches Lead Nowhere for Many" (online). USA Today.com, 2003 (cited 9 April 2003). Available at http://www.gt-cybersource.org.

———. "Some Can Sail Over High School" (online). USA Today.com, 2002 (cited 15 August 2002). Available at http://www.gt-cybersource.org.

Van Tassel-Baska, Joyce. *Comprehensive Curriculum for Gifted Learners*, 2d ed. (Boston: Allyn and Bacon, 1994).

———. "Educational Decision Making on Acceleration and Ability Grouping." *Gifted Child Quarterly* 36, no. 2 (1992): 68–72.

———. "The Talent Search as an Identification Model." *Gifted Child Quarterly* 28, no. 4 (1984): 172–76.

———. "The Use of Aptitude Tests for Identifying the Gifted: The Talent Search." *Roeper Review* 8, no. 3 (1986): 185–89.

———. "What Matters in Curriculum for Gifted Learners: Reflections on Theory, Research and Practice." In *Handbook of Gifted Education*, ed. by Nicholas Colangelo and Gary Davis (Boston: Allyn and Bacon, 2003), pp. 174–83.

Van Tassel-Baska, Joyce, and Paula Oleszewski-Kubilius. *Patterns of Influence: The Home, the Self, and the School* (New York: Teachers College Press, 1989).

Vygotsky, L. S. *Mind in Society: Development of Higher Psychological Processes*, ed. by Michael Cole et al. (Cambridge, MA: Harvard University Press, 1978).

Warshaw, Meredith. "Meeting the Needs of Twice Exceptional Children" (online). Reno, NV: Davidson Institute for Talent Development, 2002 (cited 9 April 2003). Available at http://www.gt-cybersource.org.

Webb, James T., Elizabeth A. Meckstroth, and Stephanie S. Tolan. *Guiding the Gifted Child* (Scottsdale, AZ: Gifted Psychology Press, 1994).

West, Thomas. *Young Scholars' Parents Online Seminar on Giftedness and*

Dyslexia (online). Reno, NV: Davidson Institute for Talent Development, 2002 (cited 14 December, 2002). Available at www.gt-cybersource.org.

Westberg, Karen L., et al. "Professional Development Practices in Gifted Education: Results of a National Survey." *National Resource Center for the Gifted and Talented, 1998 Spring Newsletter* (1998): 3.

Wheelock, Anne. *Crossing the Tracks: How "Untracking" Can Save America's Schools* (New York: The New Press, 1992).

Whitmore, Joanne Rand. *Giftedness, Conflict, and Underachievement* (Boston: Allyn and Bacon, 1980).

———. "Re-examining the Concept of Underachievement." *Understanding Our Gifted* 2, no. 1 (1989): 7–9.

"Why Should Gifted Education Be Supported?" (online). Washington, DC: National Association of Gifted Students (cited 4 April 2003). Available at http://www.nagc.org/ParentInfo.

Williams, Joe. "Kid Genius Just Can't Get Ahead." *New York Daily News* 16 July 2003.

Winebrenner, Susan. "Special Ed or Gifted? It May Be Hard to Tell." *Highly Gifted Children* 12, no. 2 (1998). Available at http://www.www.gt-cyber source.org.

Winner, Ellen. "Exceptionally High Intelligence and Schooling." *American Psychologist* 52 (1997): 1070–81.

———. *Gifted Children: Myths and Realities*. (New York: Basic Books, 1996).

———. "The Miseducation of Our Gifted Children." *Education Week* 16, no. 7 (16 October 1996).

Wright, Beth. "Parents' Perspective of Early College Entrance for Profoundly Gifted Children" (online). Reno, NV: Davidson Institute for Talent Development, 2001 (cited 9 April 2003). Available at http://www.www.gt-cybersource.org.

Zuckerman, H. *Scientific Elite: Nobel Laureates in the United States* (New York: Free Press, 1977).